24 days of Scratch Coding

flip COMPUTING

© Flip Computing Ltd

Flip Computing Ltd

First Published in Great Britain 2023

Text copyright © Flip Computing Ltd 2023

Supplementary illustrations and designs copyright © Flip Computing Ltd via Canva.com

Screenshots in this book show the Scratch programming language. Scratch is developed by the Lifelong Kindergarten Group at the MIT Media Lab. See http://scratch.mit.edu

All rights reserved. No part of this publication may be reproduced or transmitted in any form or by any means, electronic or mechanical, including photocopying, recording, or any information storage or retrieval system, without prior permission in writing from Flip Computing Ltd.

To find out more about Flip Computing Ltd visit www.flipcomputing.com

Contents page

4	Get started
5	Day 1
7	Day 2
10	Wordsearch
11	Day 3
13	Day 4
15	Day 5
17	Day 6
20	Find the costumes
21	Day 7
23	Day 8
25	Day 9
27	Day 10
31	Day 11
33	Day 12
35	Day 13
37	Day 14
39	Day 15
41	Day 16
44	Find the stars
45	Day 17
49	Day 18
51	Day 19
55	Day 20
57	Day 21
61	Day 22
63	Day 23
66	Spot the difference
67	Day 24
71	Answers
72	What next?

Get started!

1 Complete these activities using the online **Scratch** editor

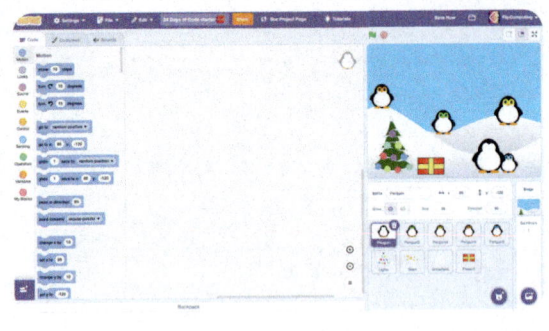

2 **Tip 1** Create a **free** Scratch account to save your project

Ask a grown up

3 **Tip 2** 'High Contrast' makes blocks easier to read

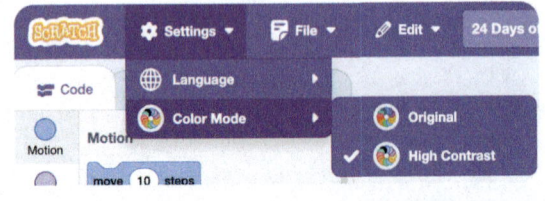

4 **Tip 3** Full screen mode is great for playing your project

Find **five** elves in this book

Day 1 - Chirp

Day 1 - Chirp

1 Open the starter project
https://flipcomputing.com/scratch24
Click 'Remix' to save your copy

2 Click on Penguin sprite below Stage

3 Click 'Code' tab

Drag code blocks

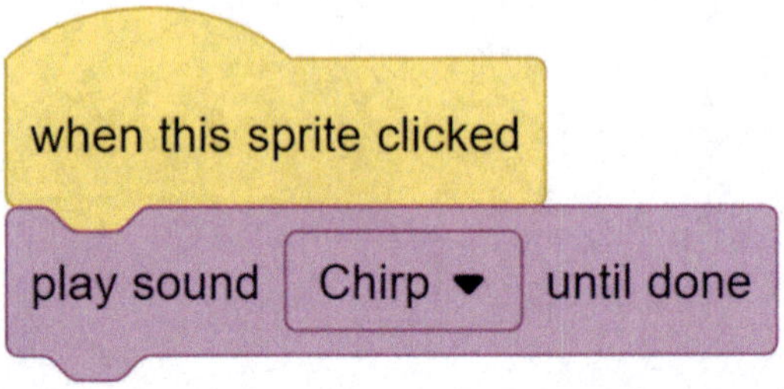

```
when this sprite clicked
play sound Chirp until done
```

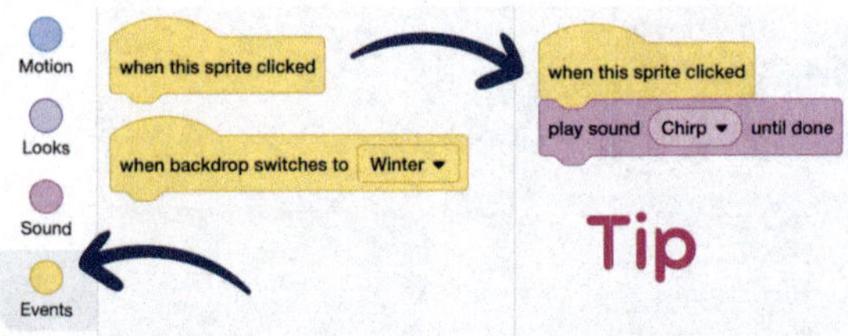

Tip

4 Click Penguin on the Stage

Hear Penguin chirp!

6

Day 2 - Northern lights

Day 2 - Northern Lights

1

Click **Backdrops 1**

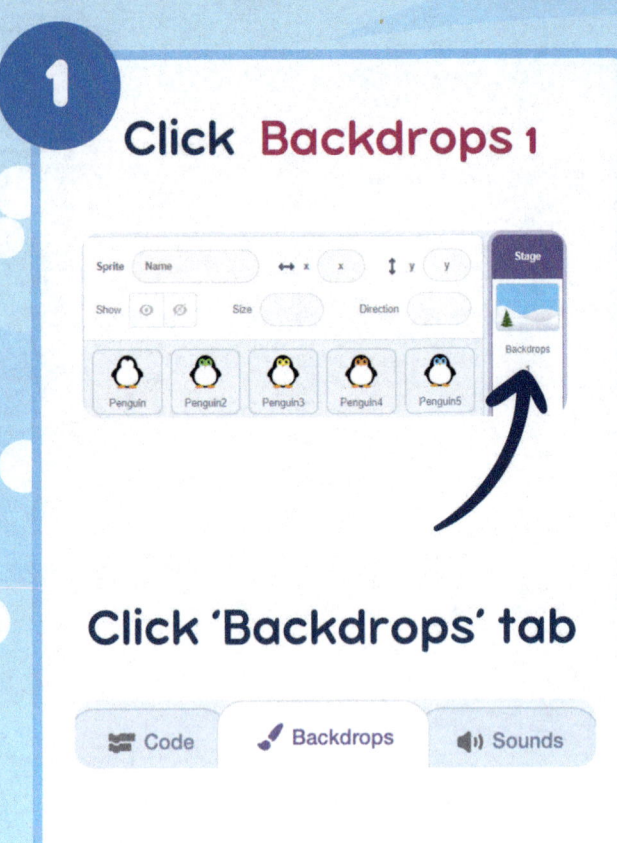

Click 'Backdrops' tab

2

Click on the blue sky rectangle

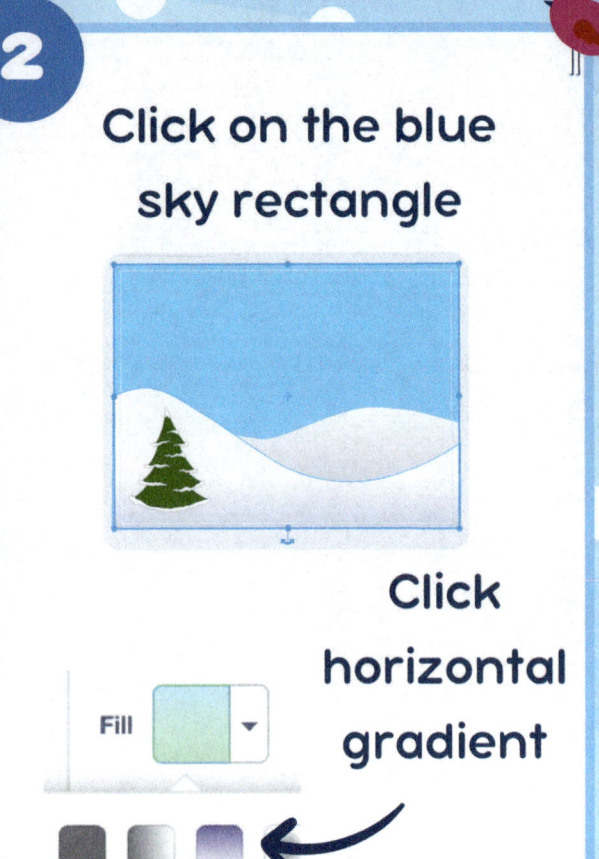

Click horizontal gradient

3

Set colours

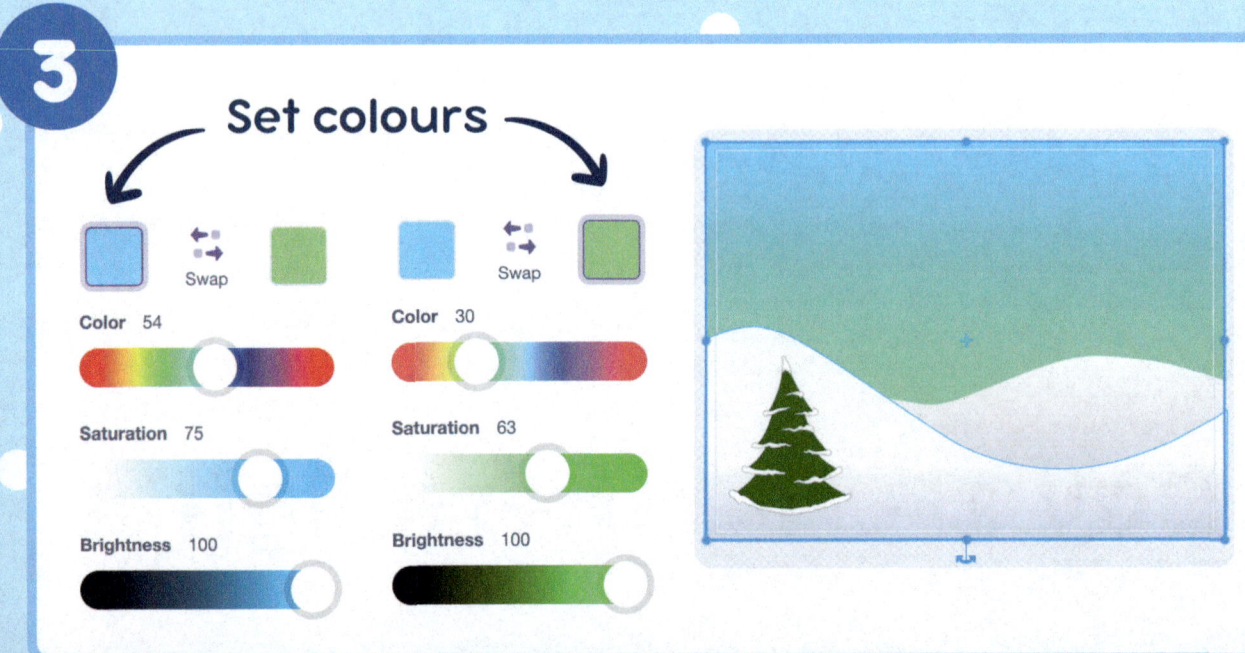

Day 2 - Northern Lights

4
Right-click (tap and hold) to duplicate the backdrop

Click on the sky

5
Set second colour

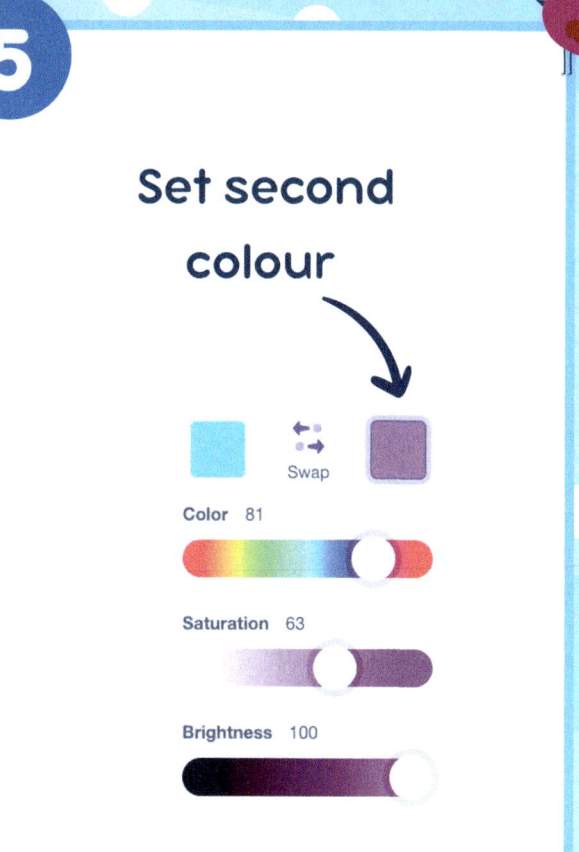

6
Add code to 'Code' tab

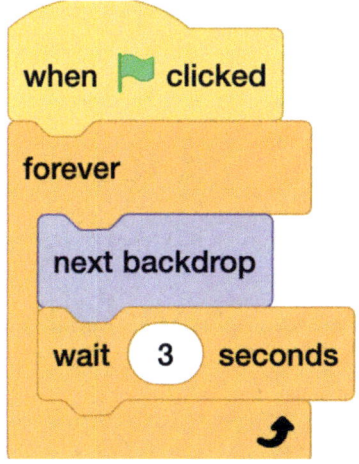

You can **choose** a different number

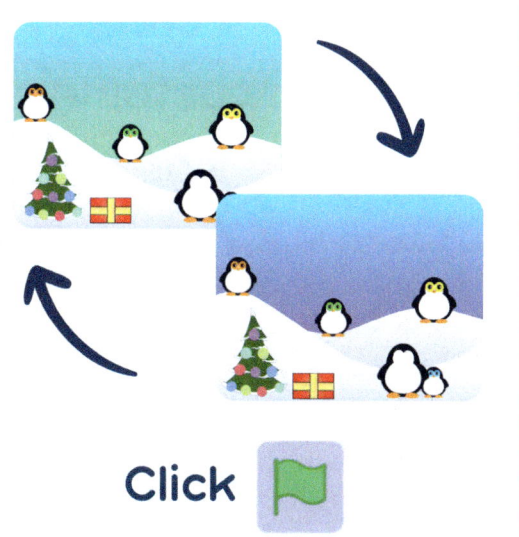

Click 🟢

Day 2 - Wordsearch

```
E G N I S N E S E D D Y
R Q A Z L M W C D H Z B
S E J R U K L P O D R X
N Q P T E I Y A C B Y M
O P S E C T S P R I T E
W O E K A D N A Q J O E
C R L S T T N I R S G W
L D K S K D Y X W A M W
B K R J O N Q V T T V Y
S C A M Q O L S K I F A
U A P E N G U I N V Z K
W B S E H T C E J O R P
```

winter   backdrop
code   stage
costume   penguin
sprite   snow
repeat   random
click   sensing
project   sparkle

Answers on page 71

10

Day 3 - Drag a star

Day 3 - Drag a star

1 Click add sprite

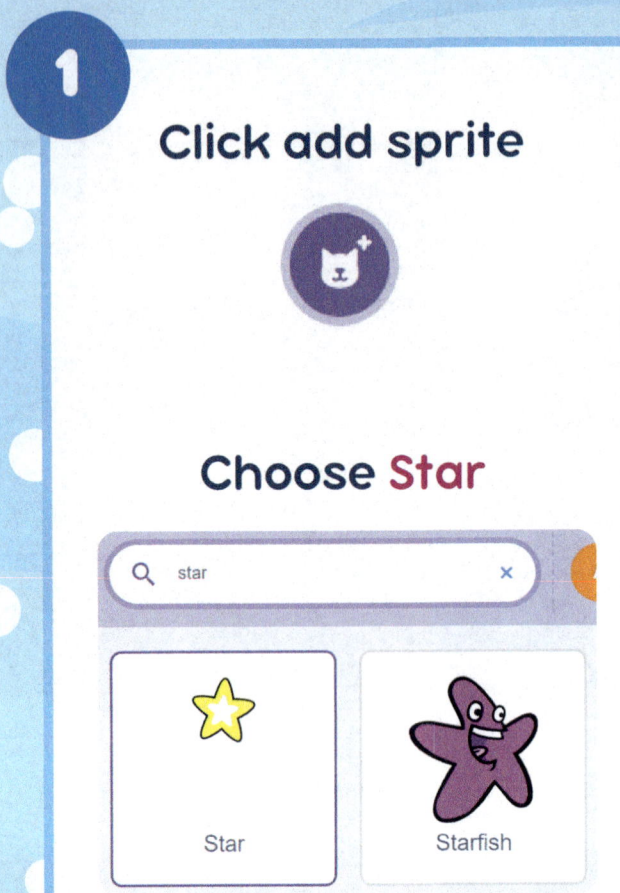

Choose Star

2 Drag Star into position on Stage

3 Click 'Full screen'

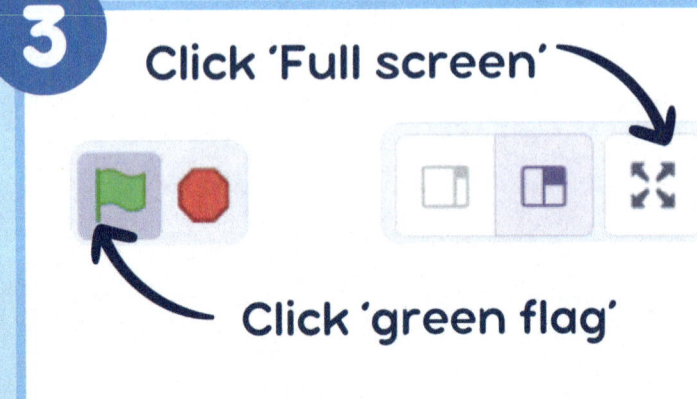

Click 'green flag'

Drag the star

Click 'green flag' to drag again.
When finished, click 'not Full screen'

Day 4 - Jump!

Day 4 – Jump!

1. Select Penguin2

Click 'Costumes' tab
Right-click, 'duplicate'

Flip wings

2. Click 'Sounds' tab

Add sound **Boing**

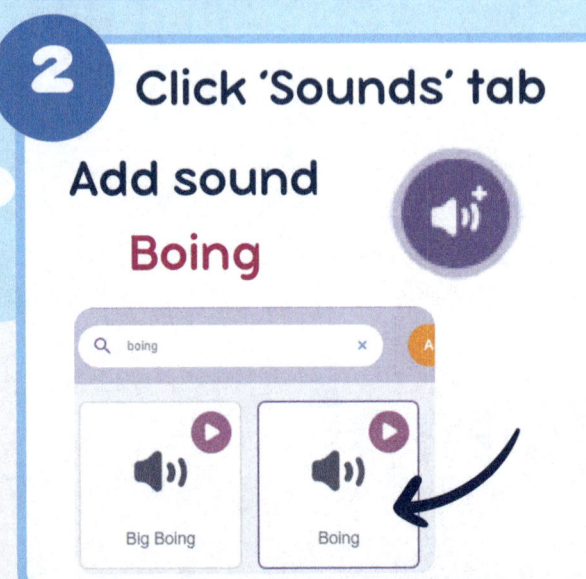

3. Add code to jump

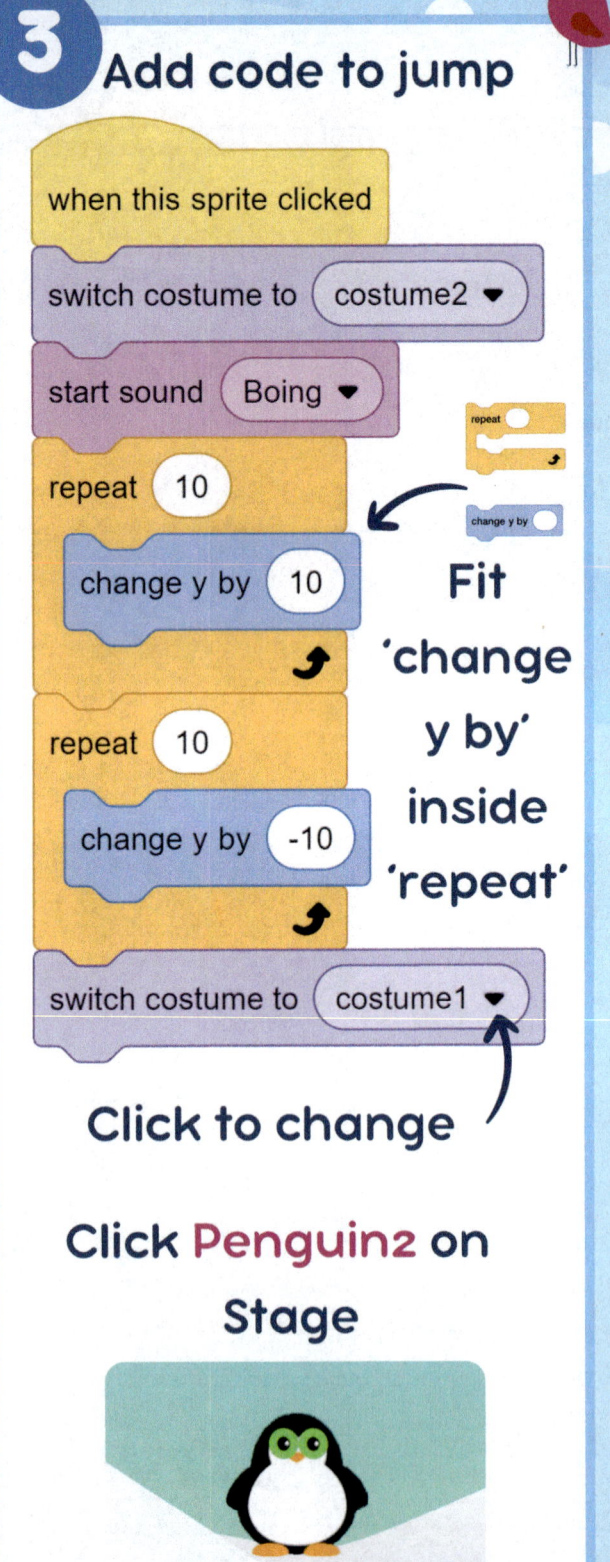

Fit 'change y by' inside 'repeat'

Click to change

Click **Penguin2** on Stage

Day 5 - I ♥ winter

Day 5 - I ♥ winter

1
Select Penguin3

Add code

when this sprite clicked
say Winter for 2 seconds

2
Write a winter message.

when this sprite clicked
say I ♥ winter for 2 seconds
— emoji

3
To type emoji

Windows
 + Dot (.)

Mac
CTRL + CMD + SPACE

4
Click your sprite on the Stage

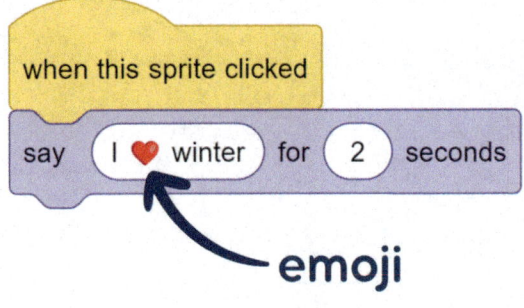

16

Day 6 - Draw a face

Day 6 - Draw a face

1 Click the **Penguin** sprite

Click 'Costumes' tab

2  Click circle tool

Set orange fill and no outline. **Tip** Brightness 100.

Draw a circle

3 Click reshape tool

Click top point

Click 'Delete'

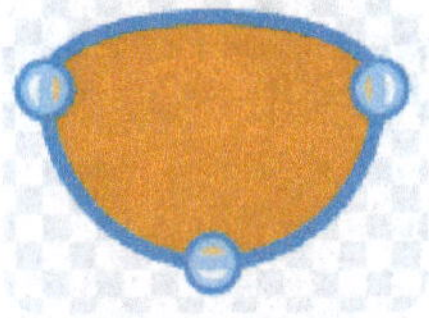

4 Click bottom point

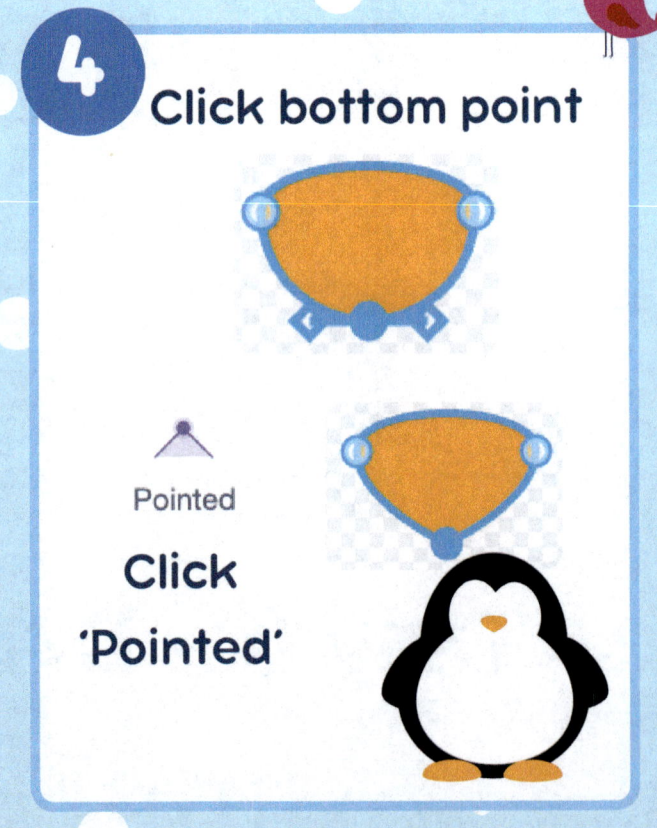

Click 'Pointed'

Day 6 - Draw a face

5 Click circle tool

Set **black** fill, **25** outline weight, and a **blue** outline

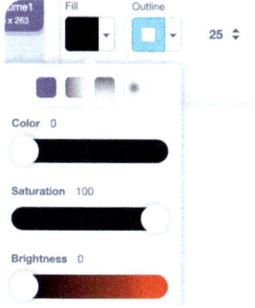

6 Draw a circle

Set white fill and no outline

Draw a small circle

7 Click select tool

Shift-click both circles

Click 'Copy' then 'Paste'

Tip: If you can't shift-click do one at a time

8 Drag to position

You can **choose** a different colour

19

Day 6 - Find the costumes

Can you find these costumes in Scratch?

Answers on page 71

20

Day 7 - Hide

Day 7 - Hide

1. Select Penguin4

Add code

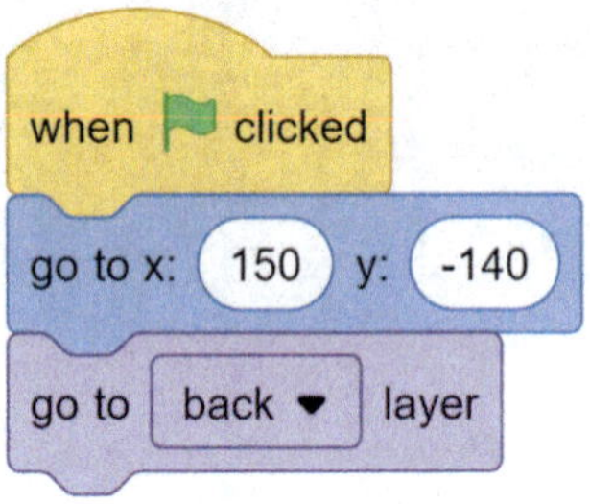

```
when [flag] clicked
go to x: 150 y: -140
go to [back ▼] layer
```

2. Add code to hide when loud

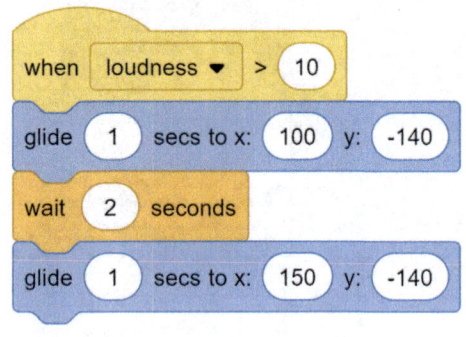

3. Tip

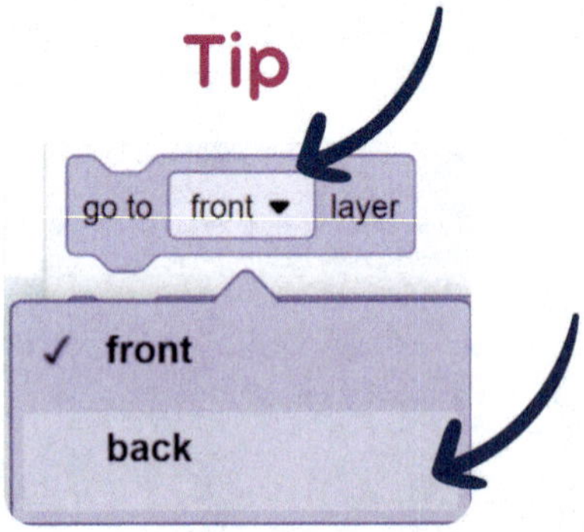

Allow microphone

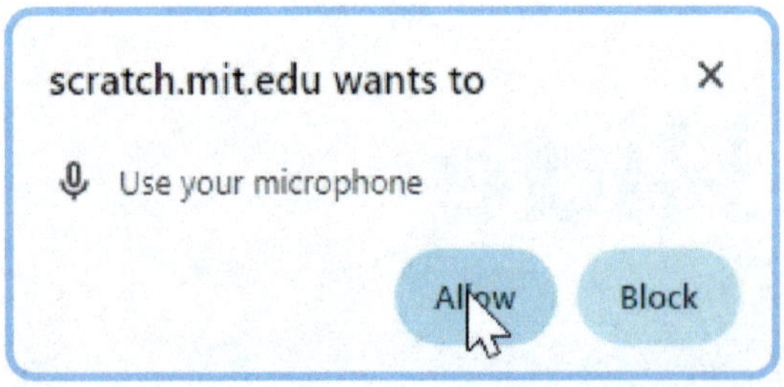

4. Make a noise!

The little penguin will hide

Day 8 - Dress up

Day 8 - Dress up

1 Select Penguin

Click 'Costumes' tab

Choose a costume

Add 'Winter Hat'

2 Click select tool

Click and drag across the hat

'Group' then 'Copy'

Group   Copy

3

Click costume1

Click 'Paste'

Paste

Position and resize

Repeat for Scarf-a

24

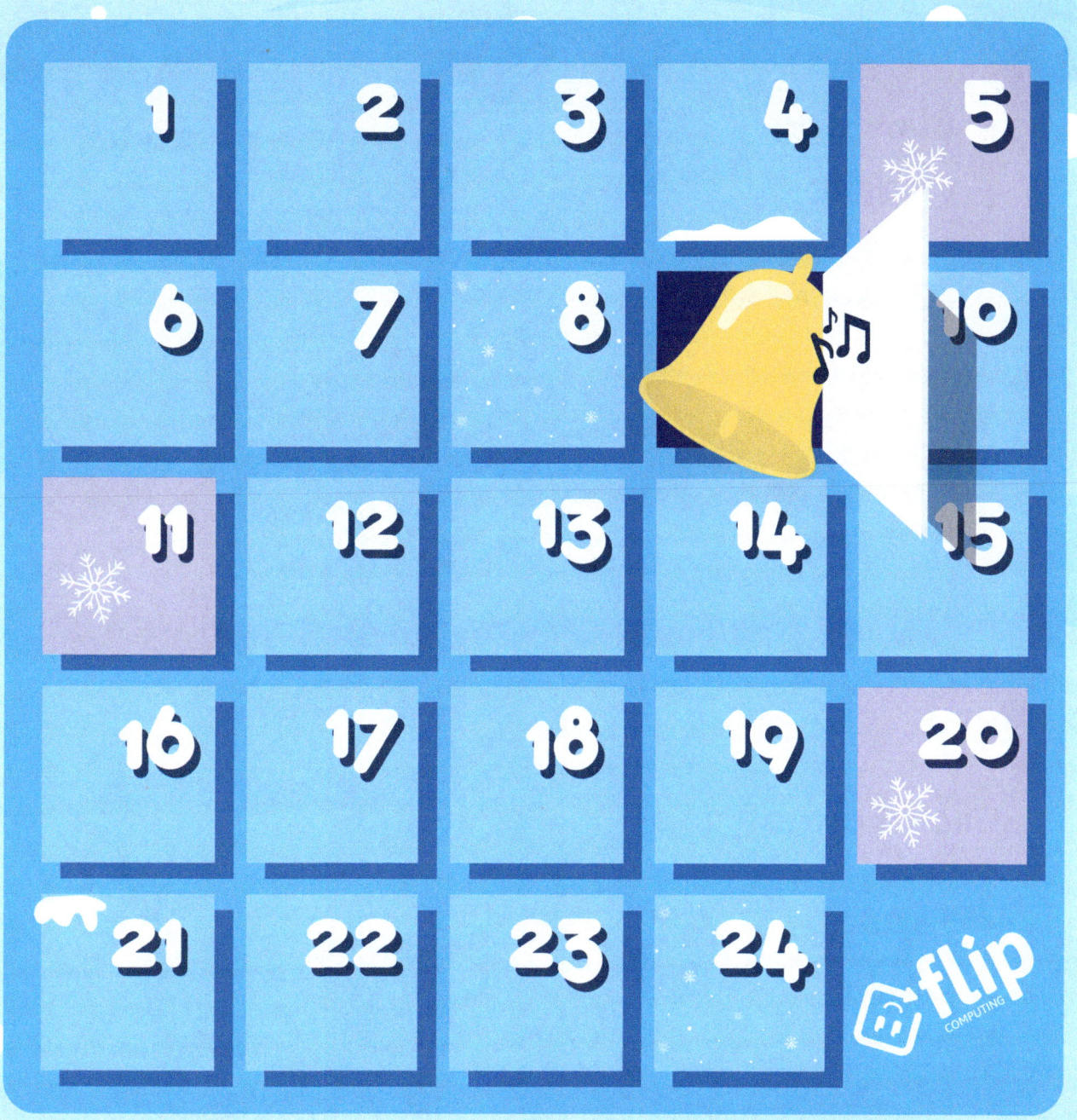

Day 9 - Music

Day 9 - Music

1

Click add sprite

Choose **Bell**

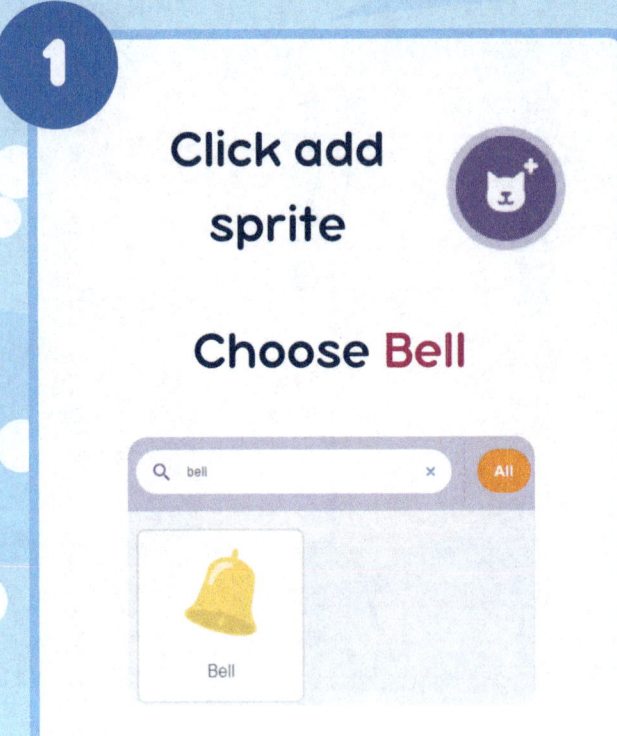

2

Click 'Sounds' tab

Add sound **Chill**

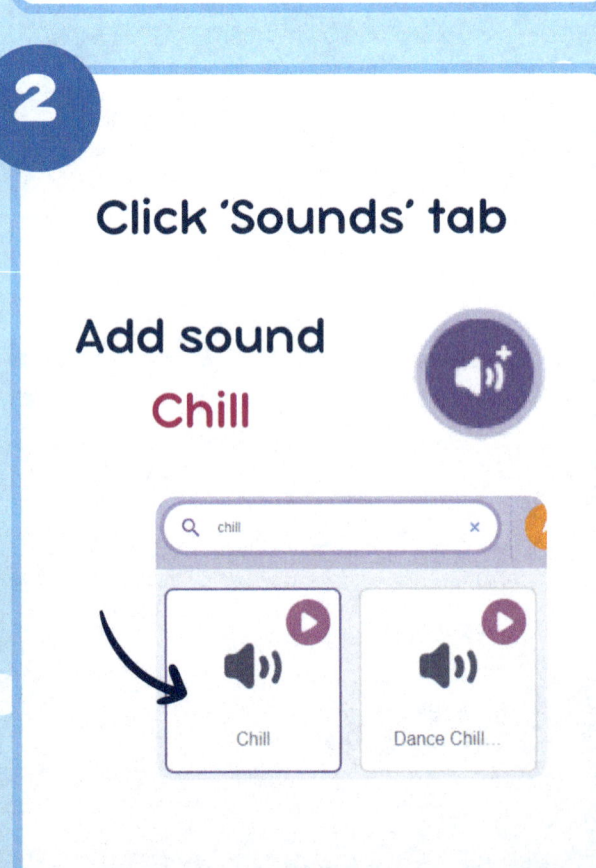

3 Add code

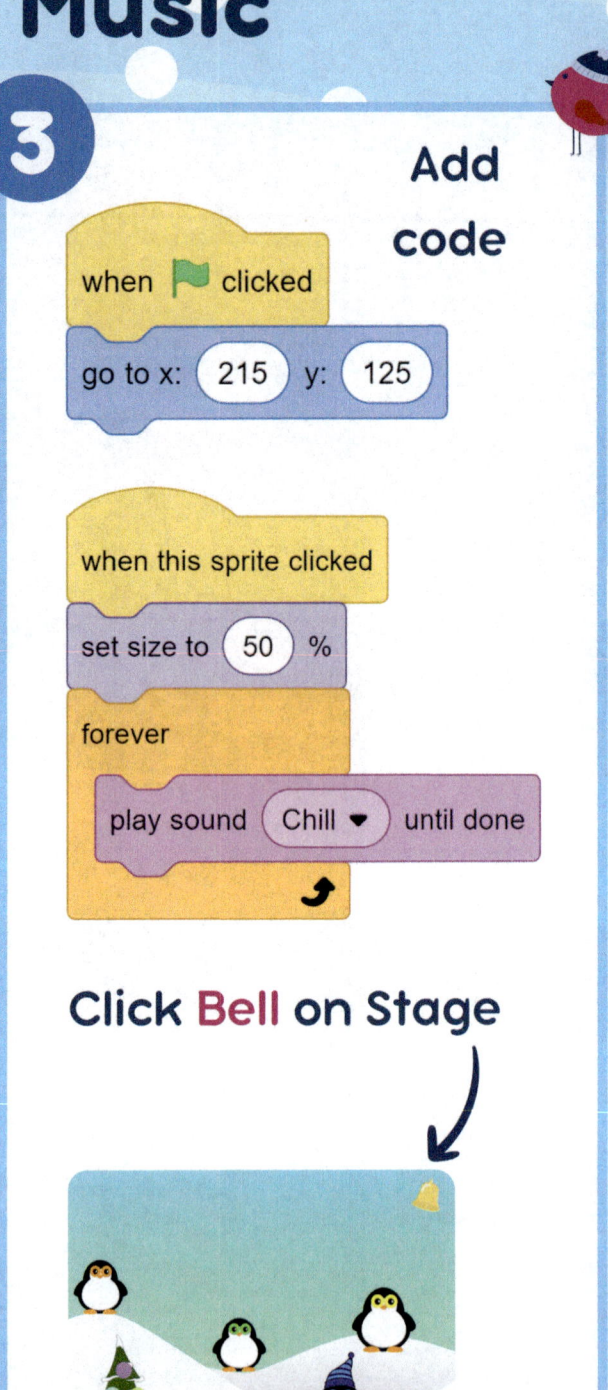

Click **Bell** on Stage

Click 'Stop' to stop music

Day 10 - Draw a balloon

Day 10 - Draw a balloon

1 Paint a sprite

Name it **Balloon**

Click 'Costumes' tab

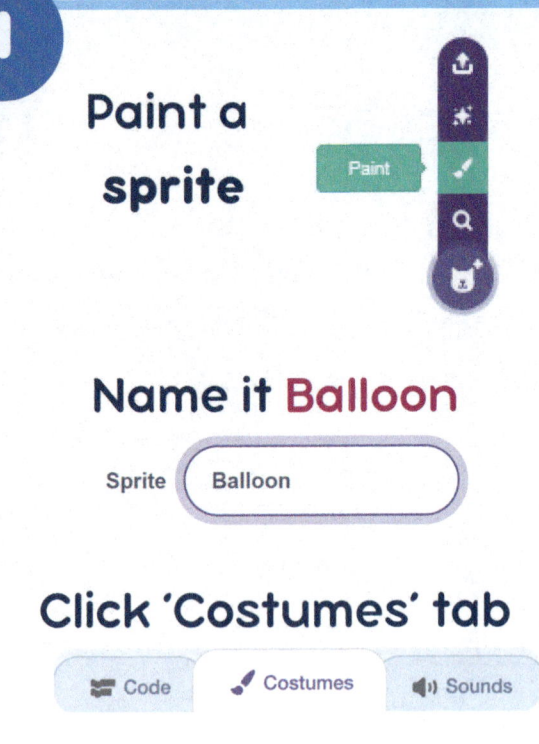

2 Click circle tool

Set **red** fill, **4** outline weight

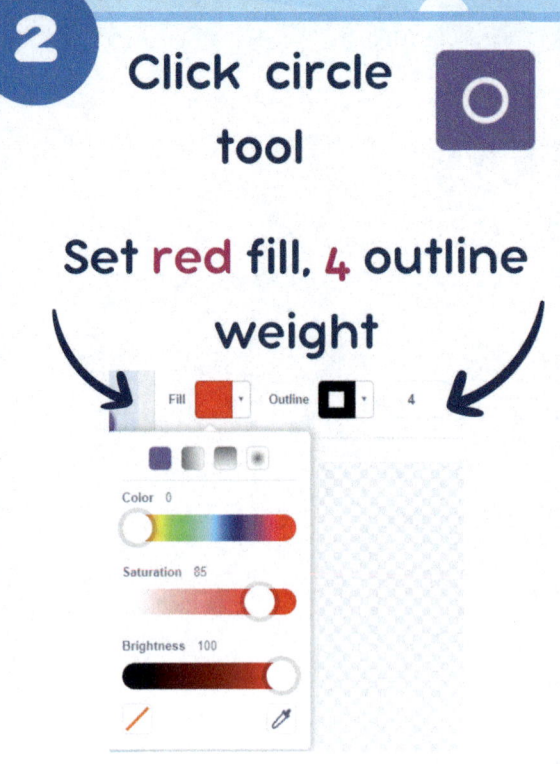

3 Shift-click to draw a big circle

Draw a small ellipse

4 Click select tool

Position ellipse

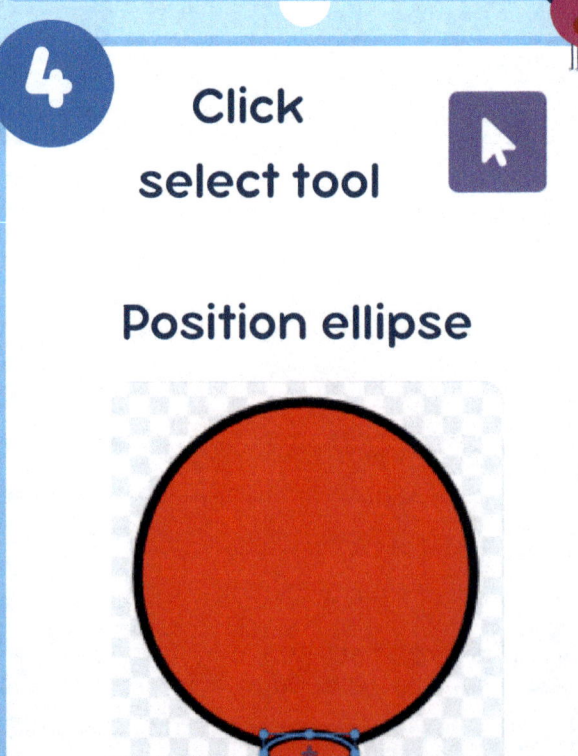

28

Day 10 - Draw a balloon

5

Click on big circle

Set radial gradient

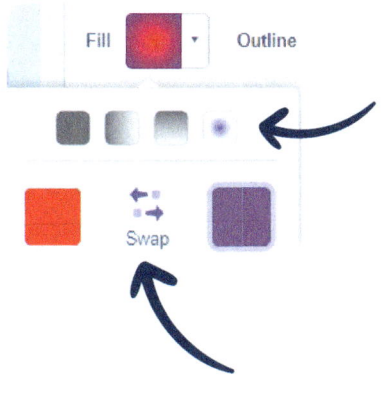

Click 'Swap'

6

Click first colour

Set Color 0
Set Saturation 50

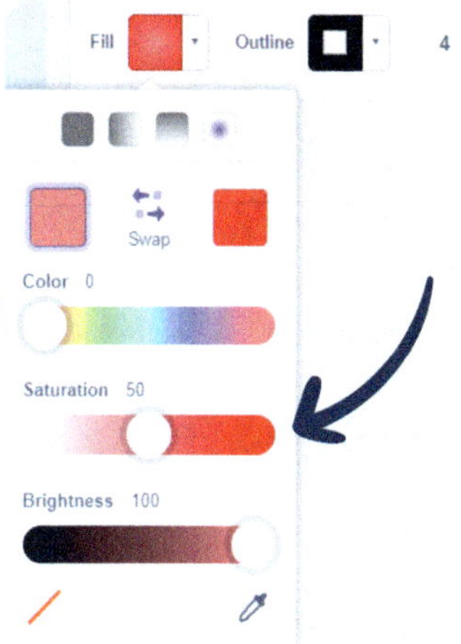

7

Click paint

Set colour black, size 10

Draw a string

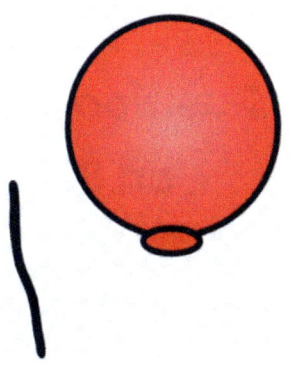

Day 10 - Draw a balloon

8 Click select tool

Move string

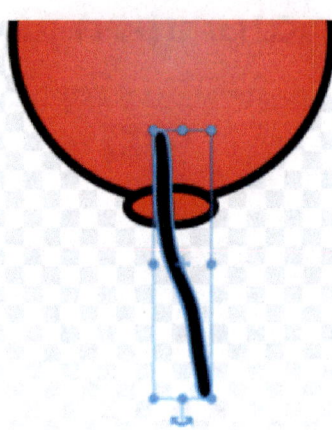

Click 'Back'

9 Select Penguin

Select left wing

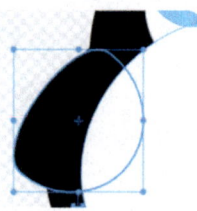

Click 'Flip Vertical'

10 Position Balloon on Stage

30

Day 11 - Starry night

Day 11 - Starry night

1
Select **Stars**

Tip some blocks have drop down menus

2
Add code to show stars after 4pm

These 3 blocks sit inside each other

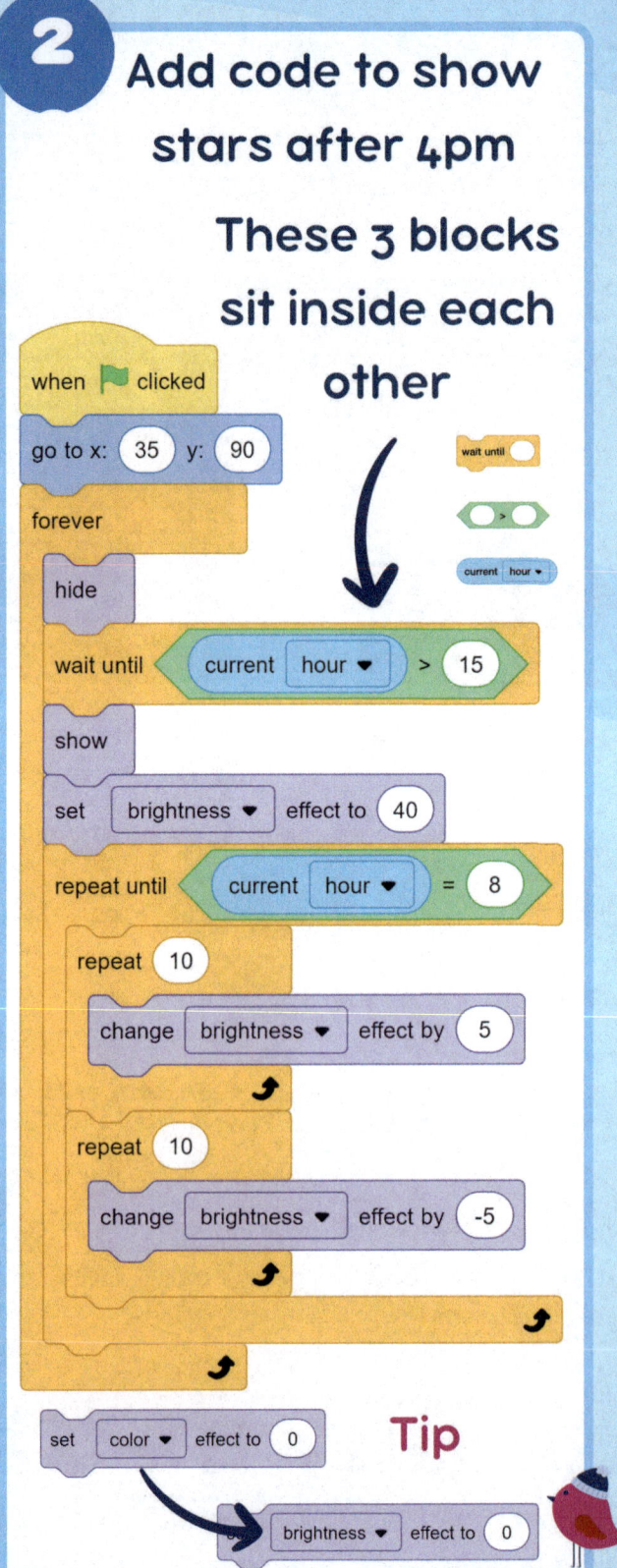

Tip

3
Click 🚩

Stars will only appear after **4pm**

Day 12 - Slide

Day 12 - Slide

1
Select Penguin5

Click 'Costumes' tab

Duplicate costume

Shift-click wings

Click 'Flip Vertical'

2
Add code to slide down and back up

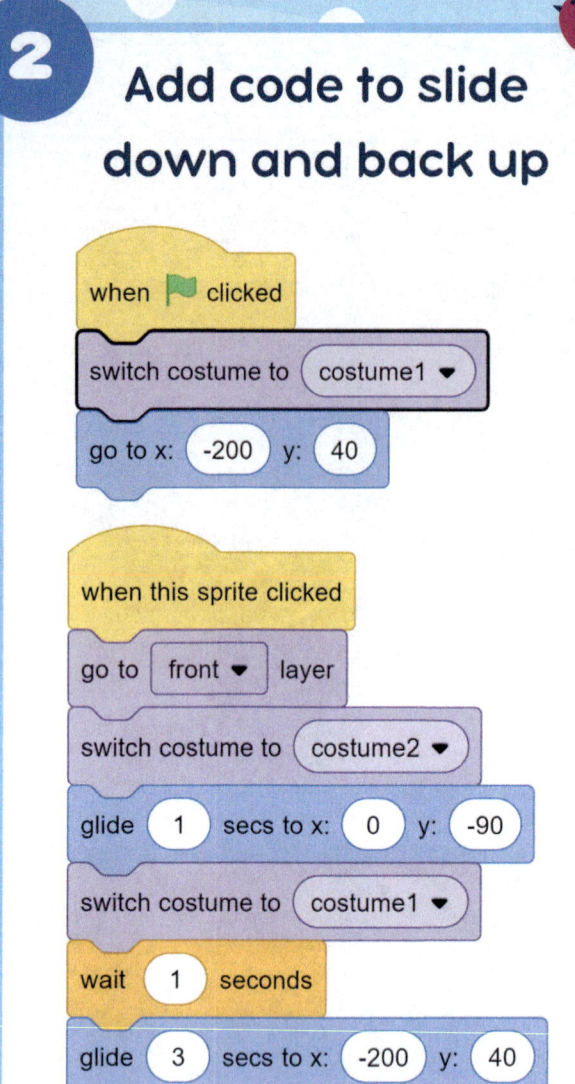

3
Click Penguin5 on Stage to slide

Day 13 - Draw a snowball

35

Day 13 - Draw a snowball

1

Click paint a sprite

Name sprite **Snowball**

Click 'Costumes' tab

Click circle tool

2

Set **radial** gradient, no outline, colour 1

3

Set colour 2

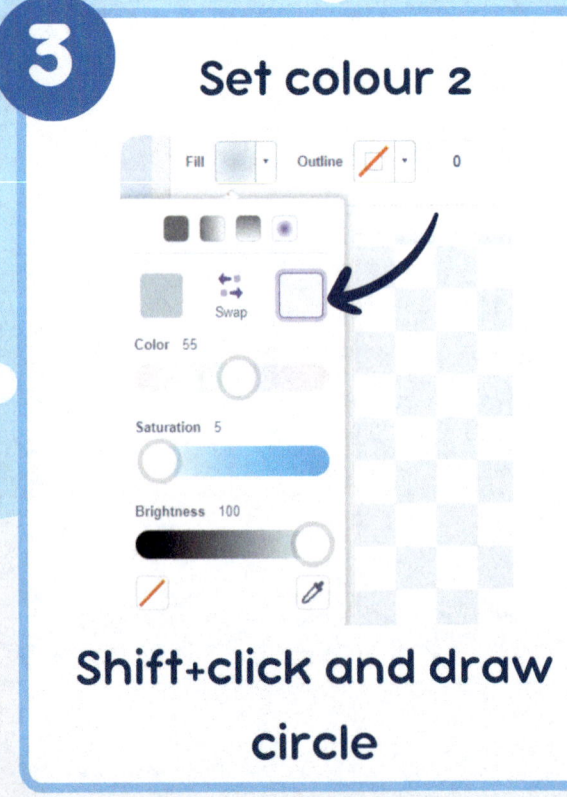

Shift+click and draw circle

4

Click reshape tool

Drag points

Position **Snowball**

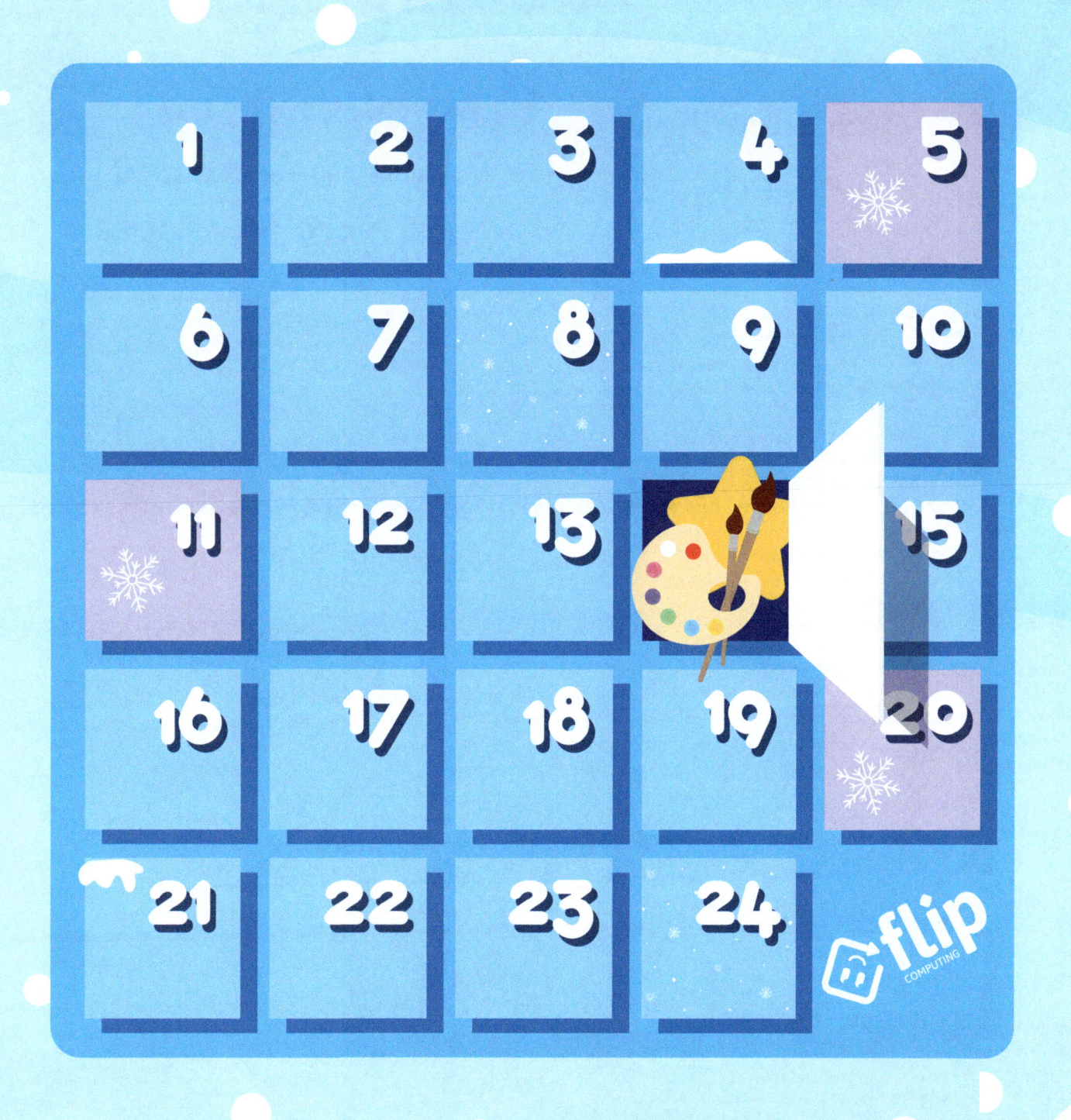

Day 14 - Shooting star

37

Day 14 - Shooting star

1 Click **Shooting star** sprite

2 Click fill in the Costumes tab and add more fill colours

3 Add code to make star shoot randomly

```
when [flag] clicked
forever
    go to x: 280 y: pick random 50 to 200
    hide
    wait pick random 5 to 15 seconds
    show
    glide 1 secs to x: -280 y: pick random 50 to 200
```

Day 15 - Find the coin

39

Day 15 - Find the coin

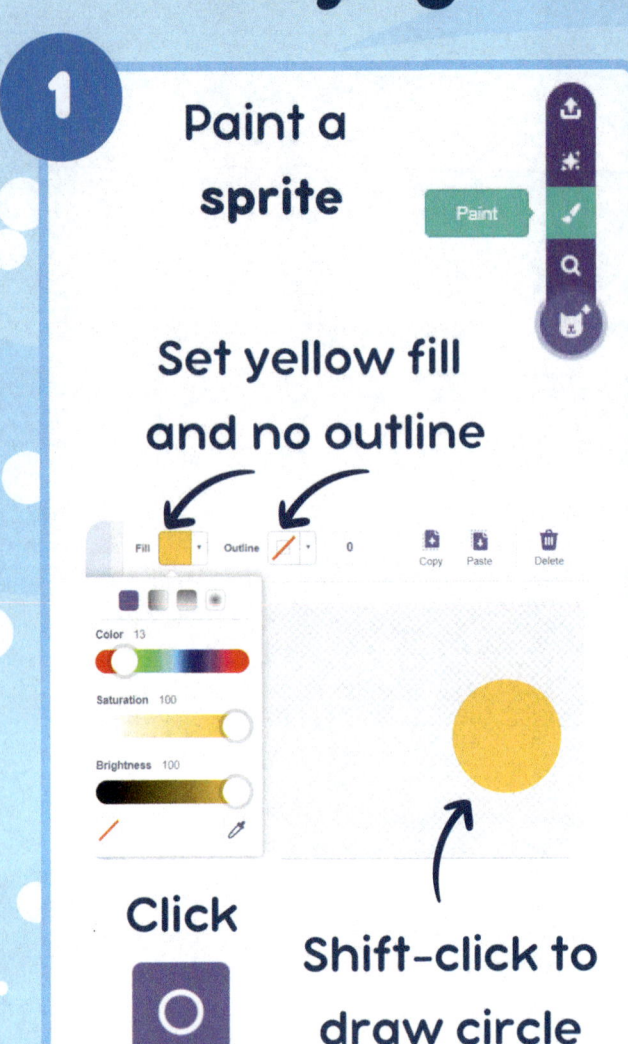

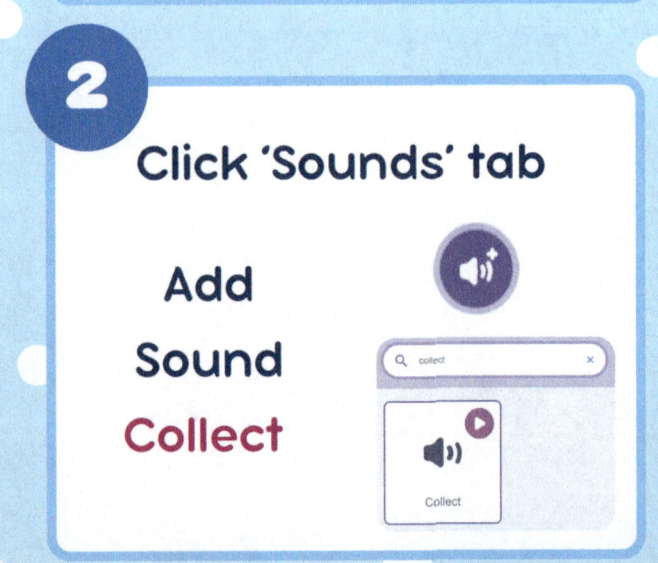

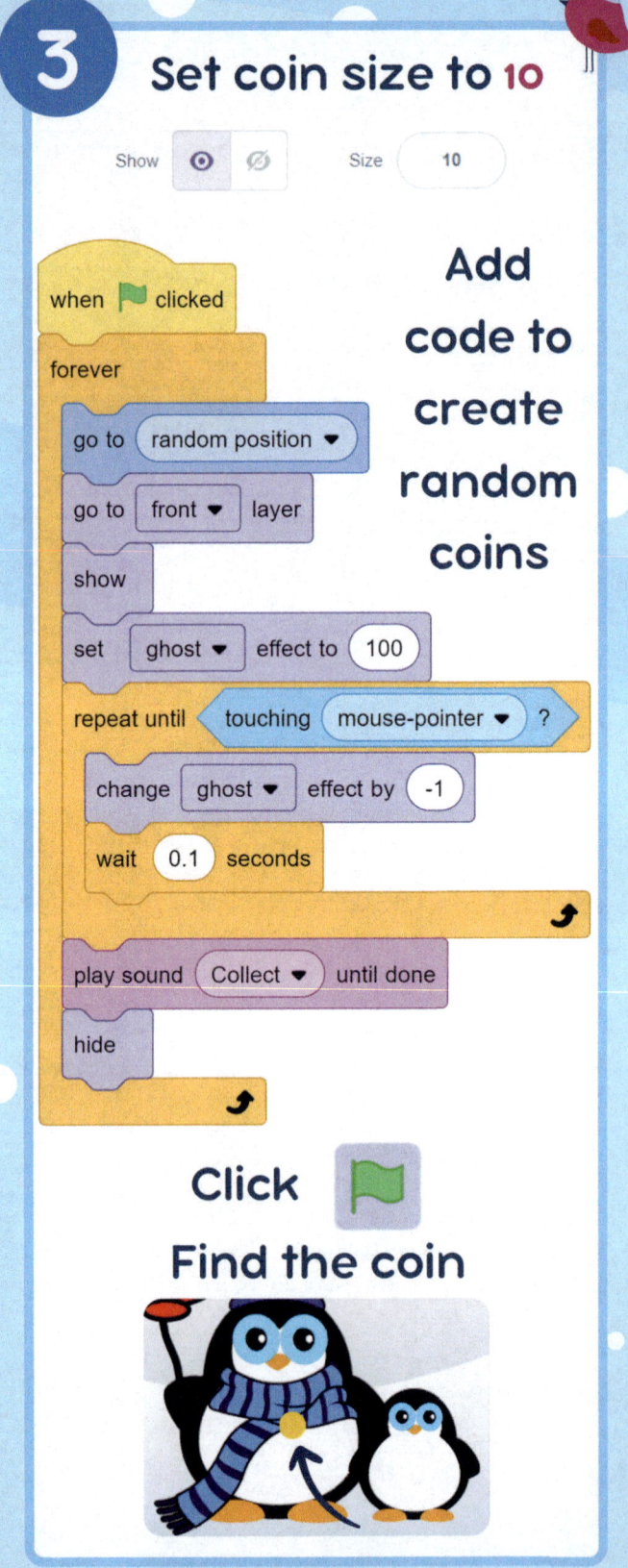

1

Paint a sprite

Set yellow fill and no outline

Click ⊙

Shift-click to draw circle

2

Click 'Sounds' tab

Add Sound **Collect**

3

Set coin size to 10

Show   Size 10

Add code to create random coins

```
when [flag] clicked
forever
    go to (random position)
    go to [front] layer
    show
    set [ghost] effect to (100)
    repeat until <touching (mouse-pointer)?>
        change [ghost] effect by (-1)
        wait (0.1) seconds
    end
    play sound (Collect) until done
    hide
end
```

Click 🚩

Find the coin

40

Day 16 - Star trail

41

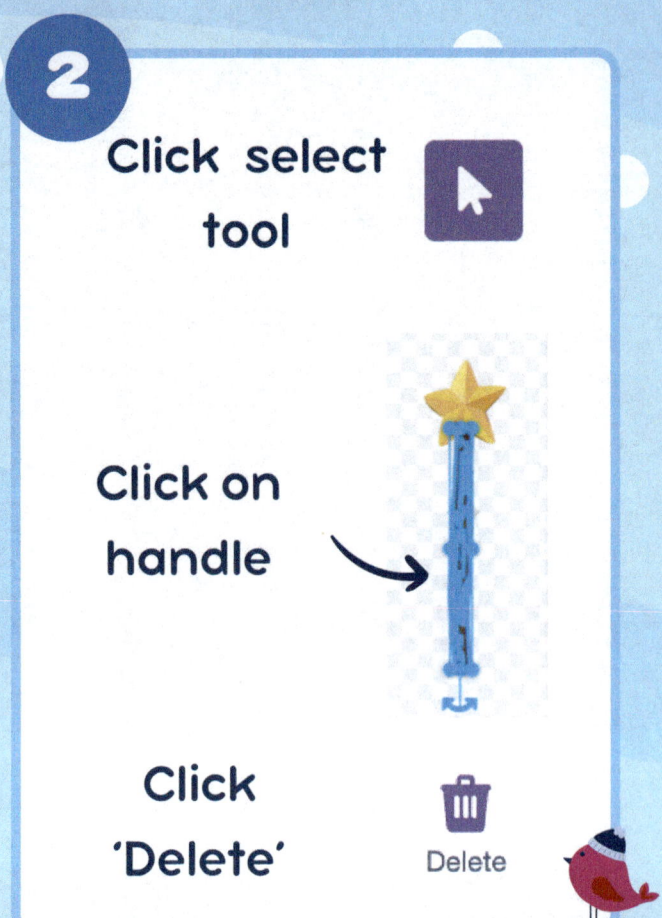

Day 16 - Star trail

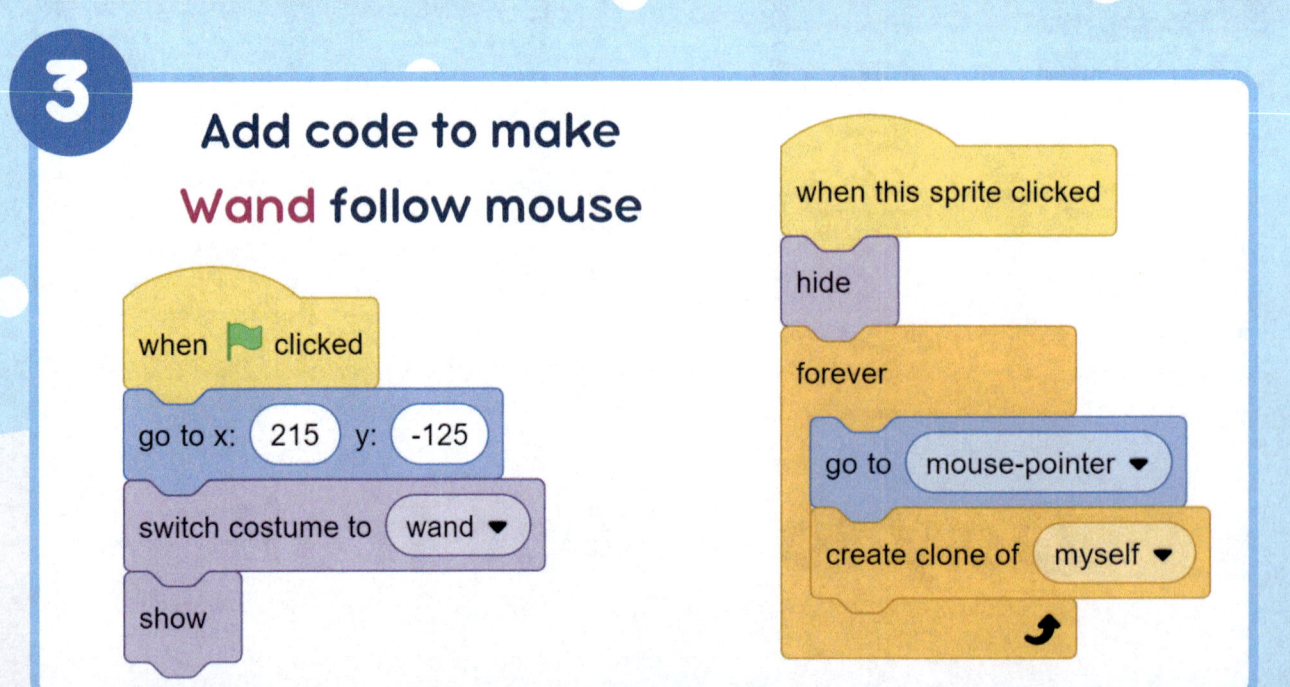

1
Add Wand sprite

Position Wand

Duplicate costume

2
Click select tool

Click on handle

Click 'Delete'

3
Add code to make Wand follow mouse

```
when ⚑ clicked
go to x: 215 y: -125
switch costume to wand
show
```

```
when this sprite clicked
hide
forever
    go to mouse-pointer
    create clone of myself
```

42

Day 16 - Star trail

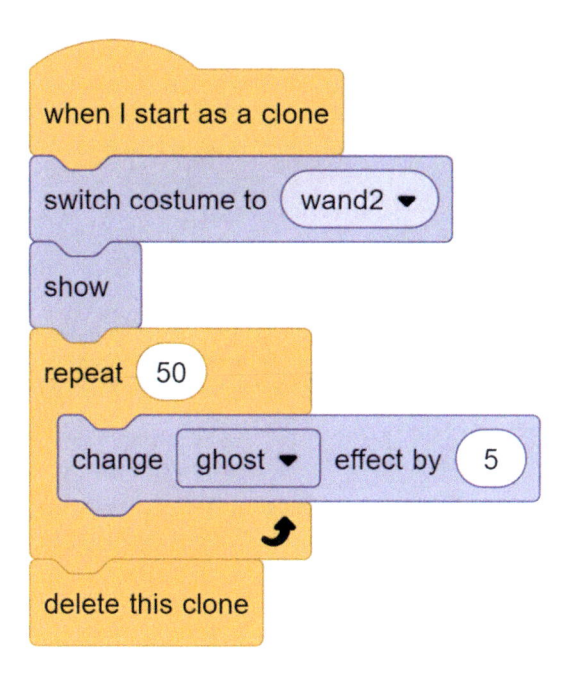

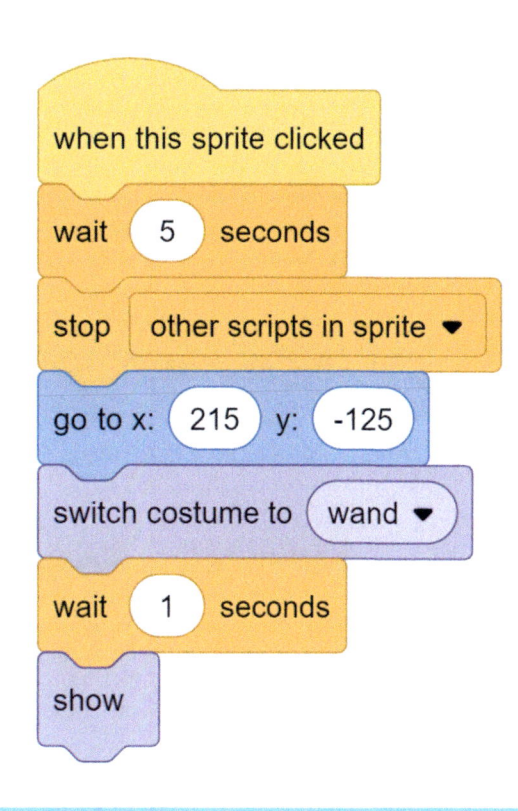

4

Add code to make trail fade (ghost) and stop

```
when I start as a clone
switch costume to (wand2)
show
repeat (50)
    change (ghost) effect by (5)
delete this clone
```

```
when this sprite clicked
wait (5) seconds
stop (other scripts in sprite)
go to x: (215) y: (-125)
switch costume to (wand)
wait (1) seconds
show
```

5

Click 🚩

Click Wand on Stage

Move around

43

Day 16 - Find the stars

Can you find these stars in Scratch **costumes** and **backdrops**?

Hint: Check the Witch House backdrop

Answers on page 71

44

Day 17 - Snowball splat

45

Day 17 - Snowball splat

1 Click the **Penguin3** sprite

Click 'Costumes' tab

Select right wing

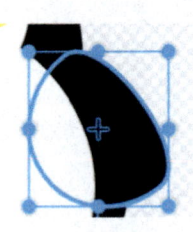

Click 'Flip Vertical'

2 Click the **Snowball** sprite

Right-click and duplicate the costume

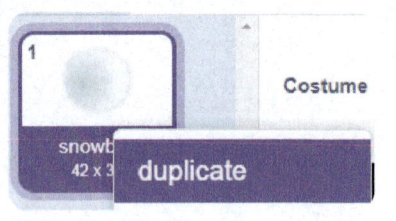

Select the snowball

3 Click 'Copy' then 'Paste'

Resize copy

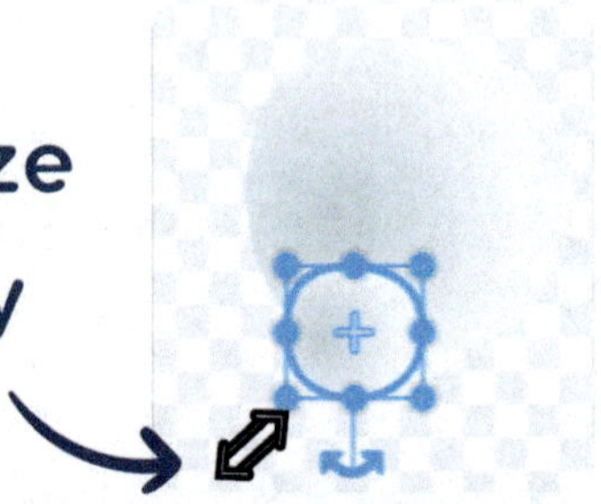

Click 'Copy' then 'Paste' 7 times

4 Drag splats around snowball

Click reshape tool

Reshape splats

Day 17 – Snowball splat

5

Click 'Sounds' tab for **Snowball**

Add Sound
High Whoosh

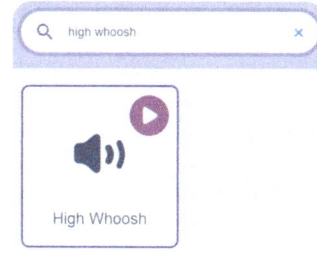

Add Sound
Crunch

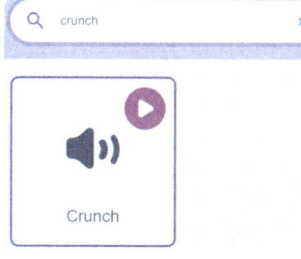

6

Add code to splat snowball

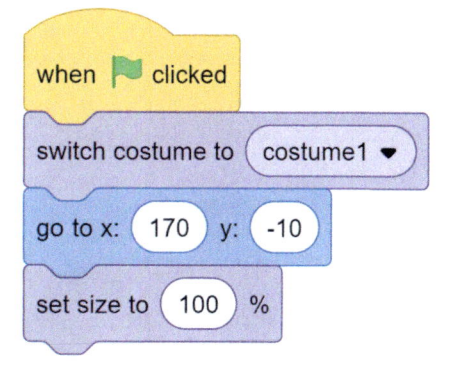

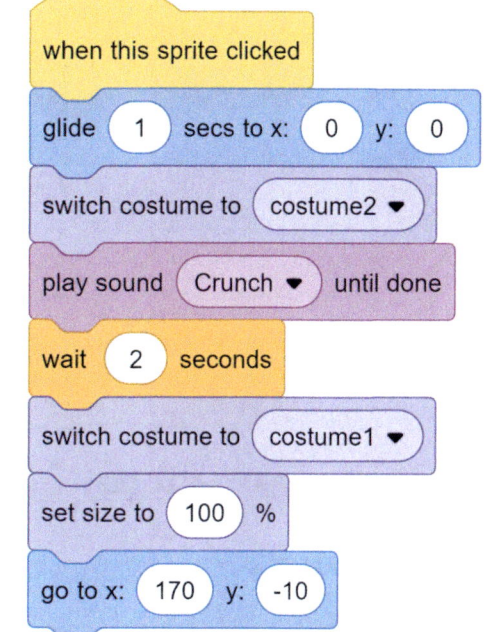

```
when 🏁 clicked
switch costume to (costume1)
go to x: (170) y: (-10)
set size to (100) %
```

```
when this sprite clicked
glide (1) secs to x: (0) y: (0)
switch costume to (costume2)
play sound (Crunch) until done
wait (2) seconds
switch costume to (costume1)
set size to (100) %
go to x: (170) y: (-10)
```

Turn over for more code…

Day 17 - Snowball splat

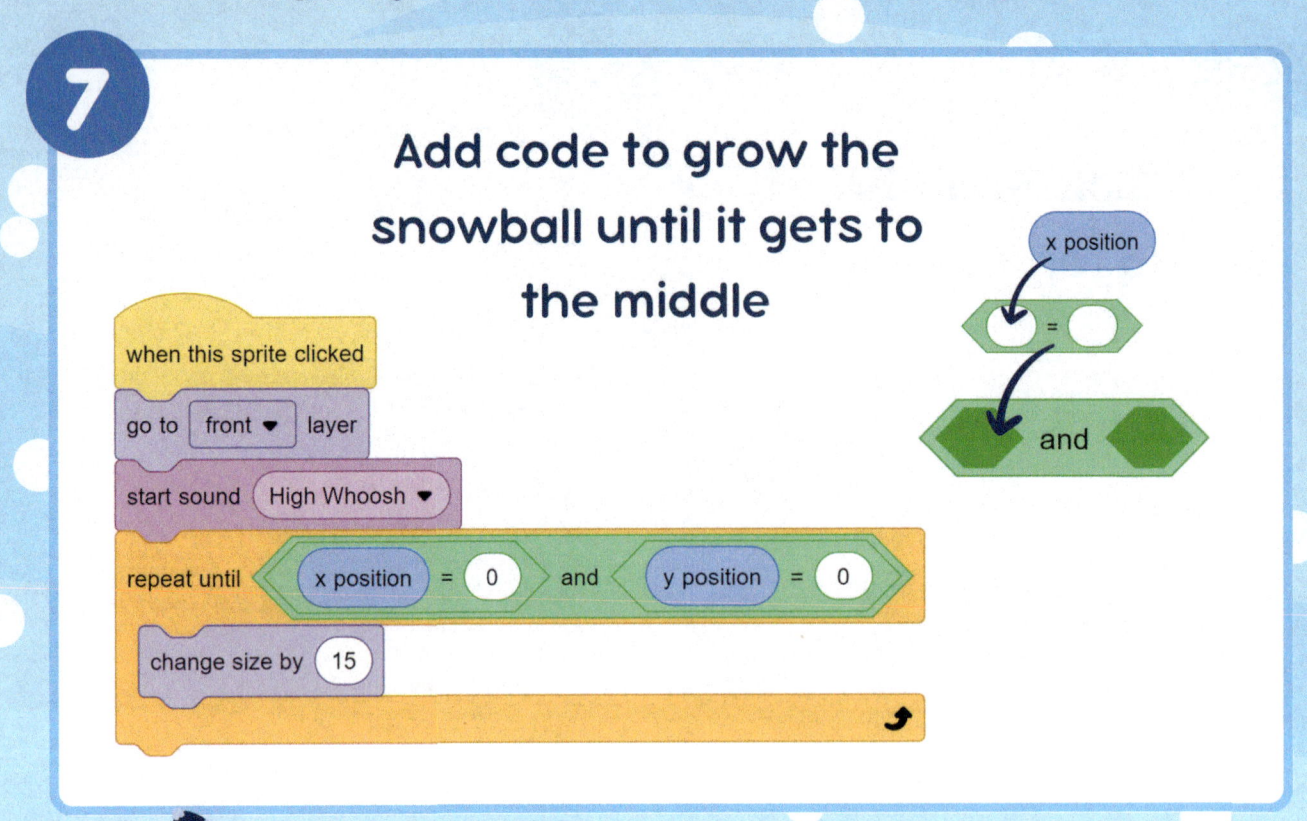

7 Add code to grow the snowball until it gets to the middle

```
when this sprite clicked
go to [front ▼] layer
start sound [High Whoosh ▼]
repeat until < (x position) = (0) and (y position) = (0) >
    change size by (15)
end
```

8 Click 🚩

Click **Snowball** on Stage

Get splatted!

48

Day 18 - Tree lights

Day 18 - Tree lights

1 Click the **Lights** sprite

2 Add code to play light patterns

```
when [flag] clicked
go to x: -150 y: -95
go to [back] layer
forever
    repeat 10
        change [color] effect by 40
        wait 1 seconds
    repeat 100
        change [color] effect by 1
        wait 0.1 seconds
    repeat 10
        set [brightness] effect to -25
        wait 1 seconds
        set [brightness] effect to 0
        wait 1 seconds
```

3 Click 🟢

Change the code to make new light patterns

50

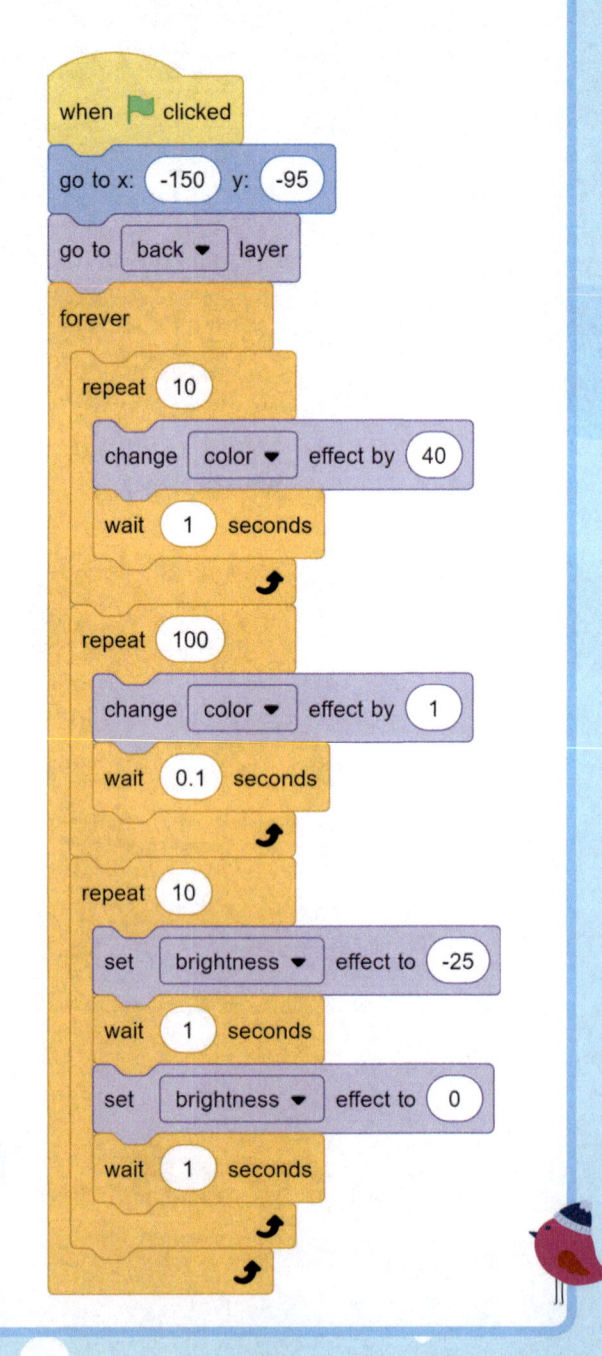

Day 19 - Draw a bow

Day 19 - Draw a bow

1

Click the **Present** sprite

Click 'Costumes' tab

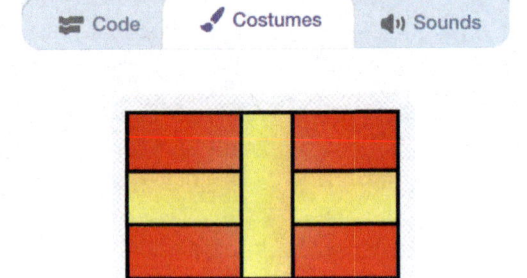

2

Click the ribbon to use the colour settings

Click square tool

3

Draw a rectangle

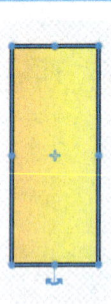

Click reshape tool

Add a point to the bottom middle

4

Drag the point up

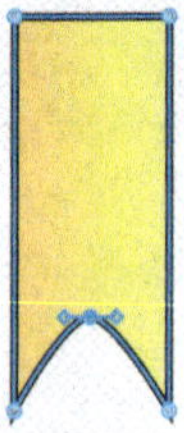

Click select tool

Rotate the shape

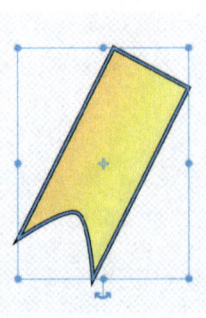

52

Day 19 - Draw a bow

5
Click square tool

Draw a square

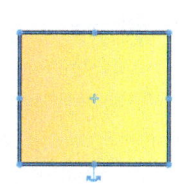

Click reshape tool

Click the top right point then 'Delete'

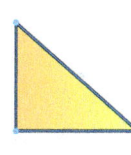

6
Drag the bottom right point up

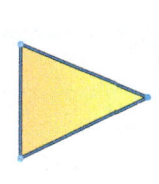

Add a point on the left

Drag the new point inwards

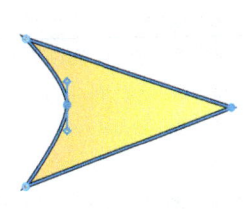

7
Click on the bottom point then 'Curved'

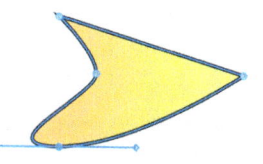

Click the top point then 'Curved'

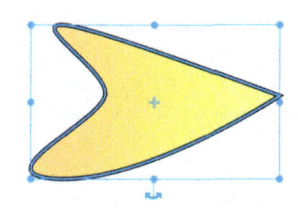

8
Click circle tool

Set black fill (brightness = 0) and draw an oval

Click select tool

Rotate the oval

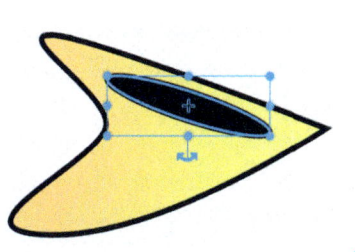

Day 19 - Draw a bow

9 Shift-click to select the shapes then drag the into position

Click 'Copy' then 'Paste'

Copy Paste

'Flip horizontal' and position

Flip Horizontal

10 Click the ribbon to use the colour settings

Click ⭕

11 Draw a circle to finish the bow

54

Day 20 - More balloons

55

Day 20 - More balloons

1

Click the **Balloon** sprite

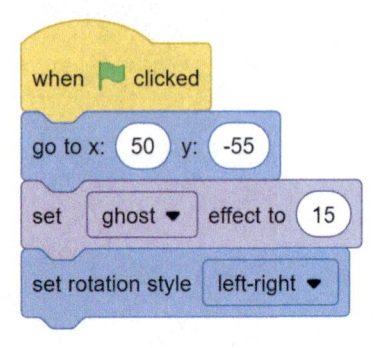

Add code to 'Code' tab

```
when [flag] clicked
go to x: 50 y: -55
set [ghost v] effect to 15
set rotation style [left-right v]
```

2

Add code to 'Code' tab

```
when this sprite clicked
create clone of [myself v]
change [color v] effect by 25
```

```
when I start as a clone
go to [front v] layer
point in direction pick random -60 to 60
repeat until <touching [edge v]?>
    move 1 steps
end
delete this clone
```

3

Tip

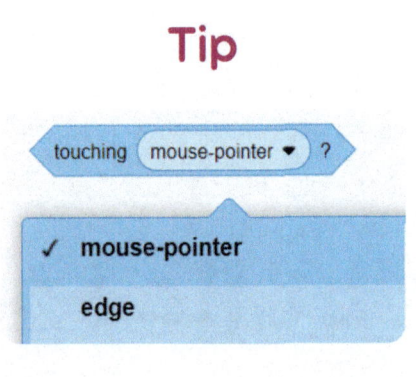

```
<touching [mouse-pointer v]?>
```

✓ mouse-pointer
edge

Click 'green flag' 🚩

Click **Balloons** on Stage

56

Day 21 - Star costumes

57

Day 21 - Star costumes

1

Click the **Star** sprite

Click 'Costumes' tab

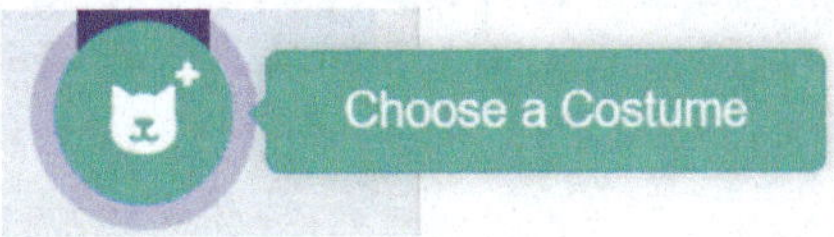

Choose **Motorcycle-a**

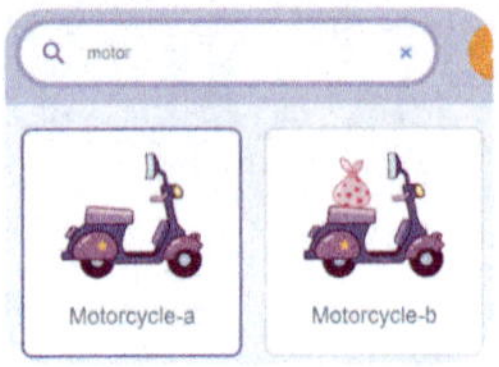

2

Select the star

Copy the star

Paint a new costume

3

Paste the star

Resize the star

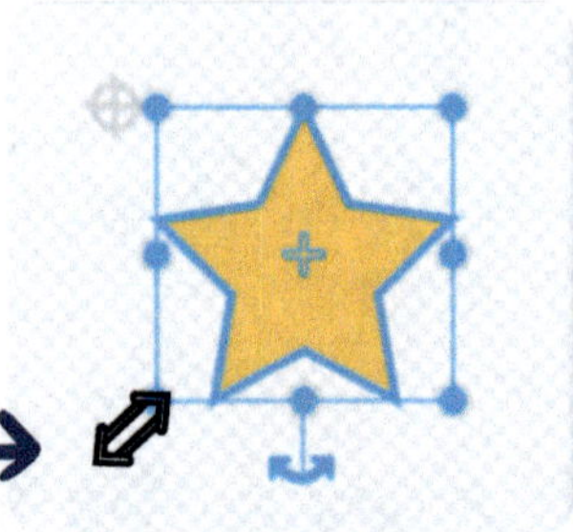

4

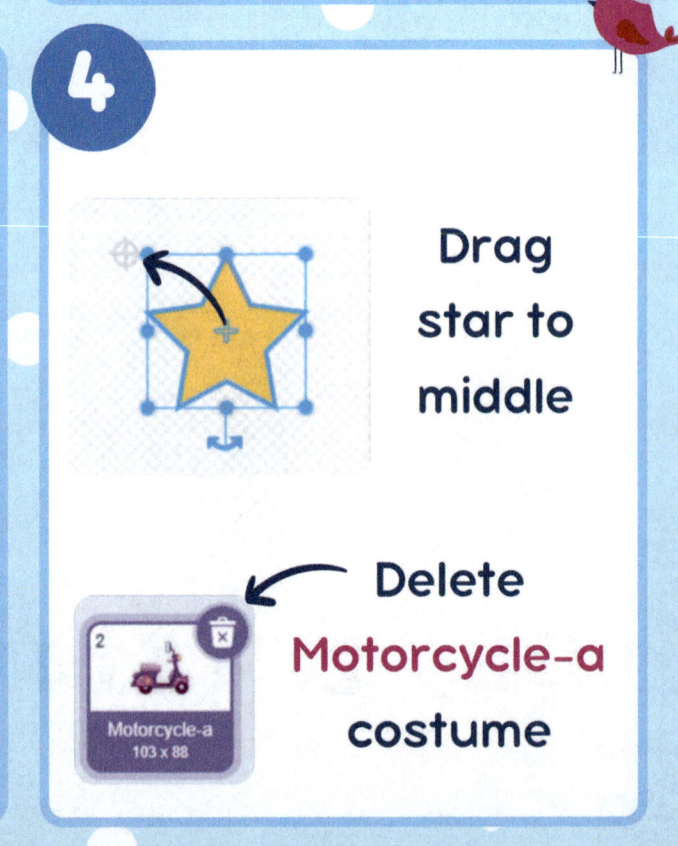

Drag star to middle

Delete **Motorcycle-a** costume

58

Day 21 - Star costumes

5. Add code to change the star costume

```
when this sprite clicked
next costume
```

Click Star on stage

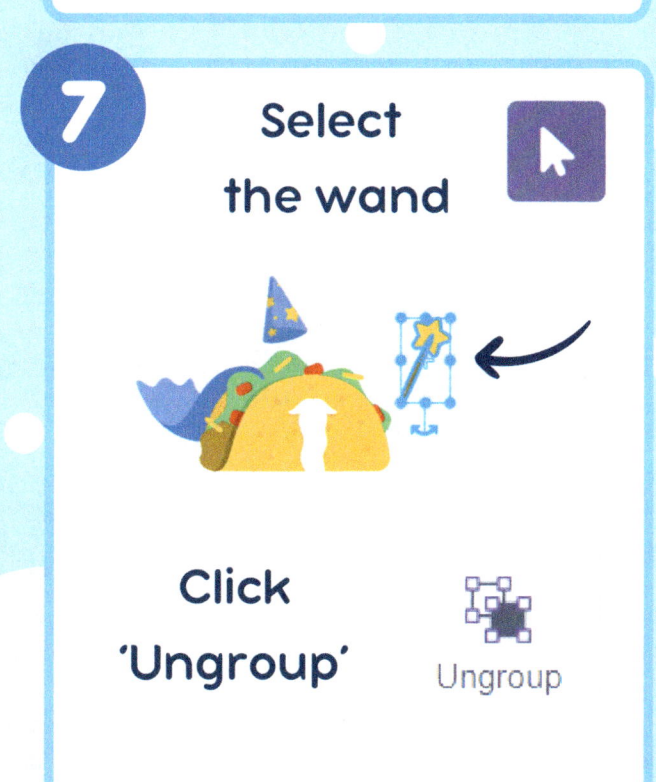

6. Click 'Costumes' tab

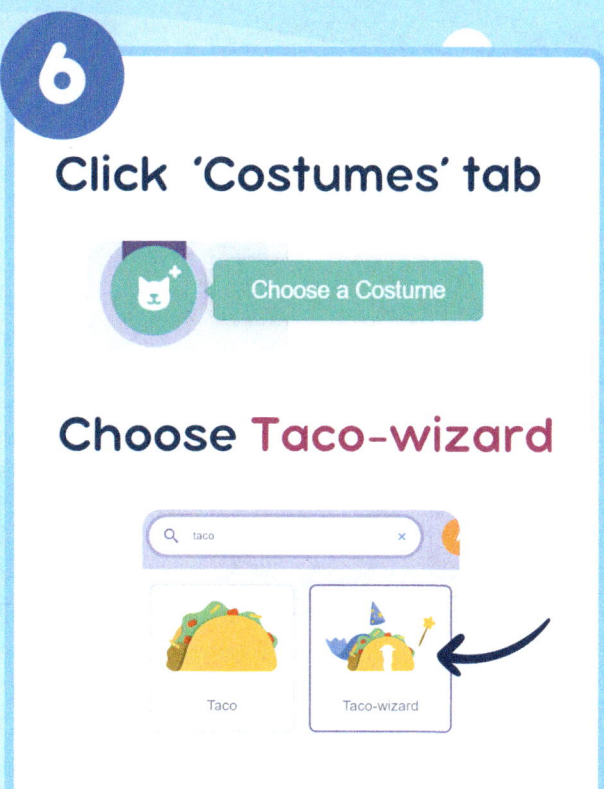

Choose a Costume

Choose Taco-wizard

taco — Taco, Taco-wizard

7. Select the wand

Click 'Ungroup'

8. Select the star

Copy

Copy the star

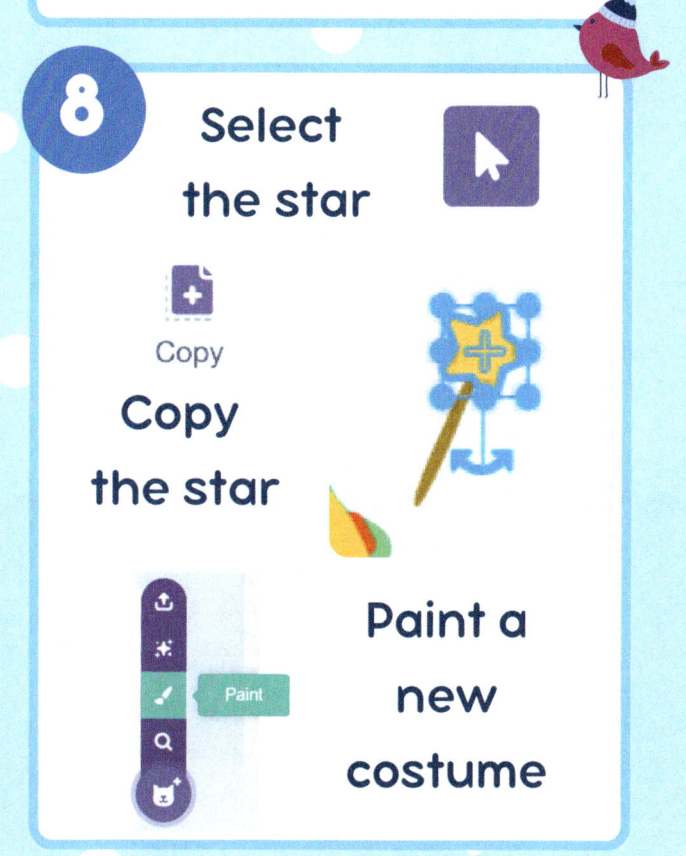

Paint

Paint a new costume

59

Day 21 - Star costumes

9
Paste the star

Resize the star

Rotate the star

10
Drag star to middle

Delete **Taco-wizard** costume

11
Drag and click star on Stage

12
Add more star costumes

Tip

You can copy and paste from some backdrops too

Day 22 - Snowflakes

61

Day 22 - Snowflakes

1 Click on the **Snowflake** sprite

Add code to create 50 clones

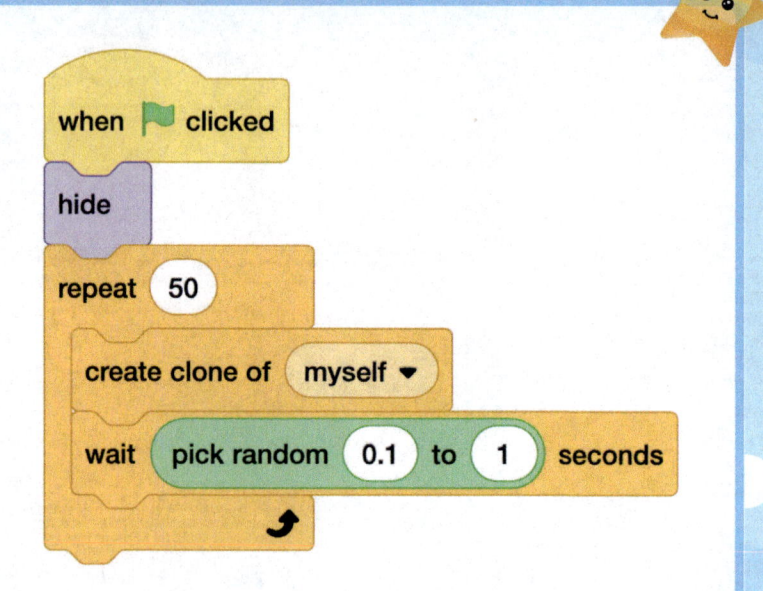

```
when [flag] clicked
hide
repeat 50
    create clone of (myself)
    wait (pick random 0.1 to 1) seconds
```

2 Add code to make the clones fall

```
when I start as a clone
go to x: (pick random -200 to 200) y: 170
go to (front) layer
show
forever
    change y by -2
    if <touching (edge)?> then
        go to x: (pick random -200 to 200) y: 170
```

3 🟩

Run your code and watch the snow

62

Day 23 - Build a snowman

63

Day 23 - Build a snowman

1 Add **Snowman** sprite

Duplicate costume

Click back to first **snowman** costume

2 Delete something

Duplicate first **snowman** costume again

3 Click **snowman** costume and delete something else.

Repeat duplicating and deleting until only 1 part left

4 Some parts are grouped together

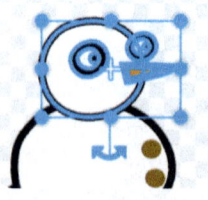

Ungroup them to delete a smaller part

64

Day 23 - Build a snowman

5
You will have lots of costumes that build a snowman

The first costume will be called **snowman**

1. snowman 68 x 53
2. snowman11 68 x 70
3. snowman10 68 x 91
4. snowman9 68 x 91
5. snowman8 68 x 91
6. snowman7 68 x 91
7. snowman6 83 x 91
8. snowman5 98 x 91
9. snowman4 98 x 108
10. snowman3 98 x 108
11. snowman2 100 x 133

This is the number of costumes you have

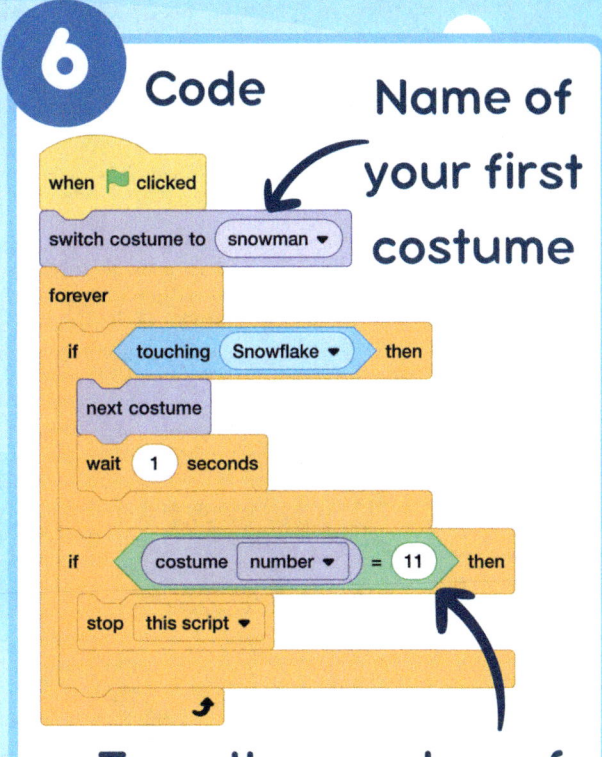

6 Code

Name of your first costume

```
when ⚑ clicked
switch costume to (snowman ▼)
forever
    if <touching (Snowflake ▼)?> then
        next costume
    wait (1) seconds
    if <(costume number ▼) = (11)> then
        stop (this script ▼)
```

Type the number of costumes you have

7 Position Snowman

Click ⚑

65

Day 23 - Spot the difference

Can you find the differences between the snowmen?

How would you create these differences in Scratch?

Answers on page 71

Day 24 - Unwrap the gift

Day 24 - Unwrap the gift

1 Go to the Present sprite then duplicate the Gift4 costume

2 Rename the costume Gift3

Costume Gift3

Click on the top parts of the bow and 'Delete'

3 Duplicate the Gift3 costume and name Gift2

Costume Gift2

'Delete' the bottom parts of the bow

4 Duplicate the Gift2 costume and name Gift1

Costume Gift1

'Delete' the ribbon

Day 24 - Unwrap the gift

5
Click on 'Choose a Costume'

Search 'Beachball'

6
Click on the **Beachball** costume

Hold down click and drag the cursor over the ball to select everything

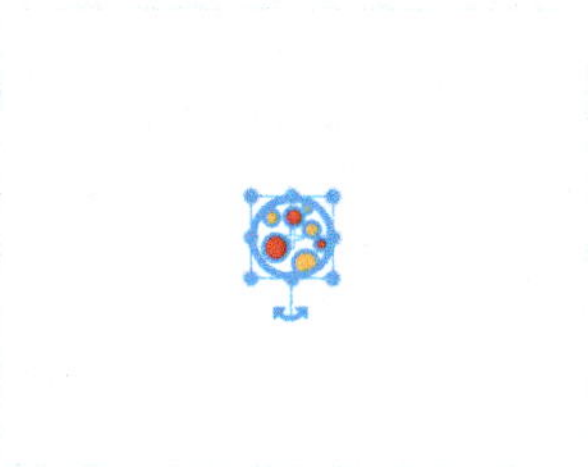

7
Drag the corners out to make the ball bigger.

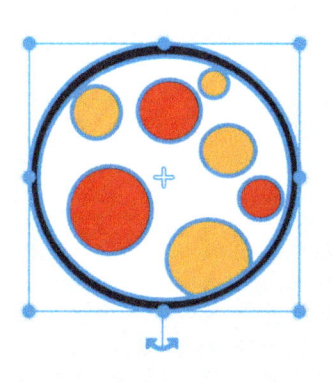

Day 24 - Unwrap the gift

8 Now you have five costumes.

The first four unwrap the present.

The last one is the gift inside.

9 Add code to start on the **Gift4** costume.

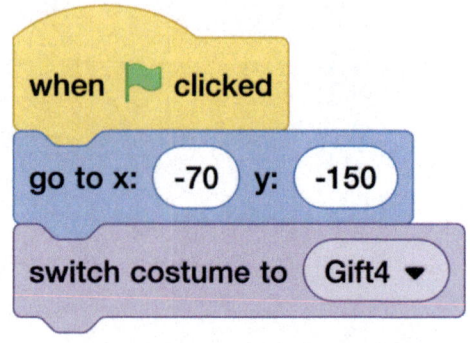

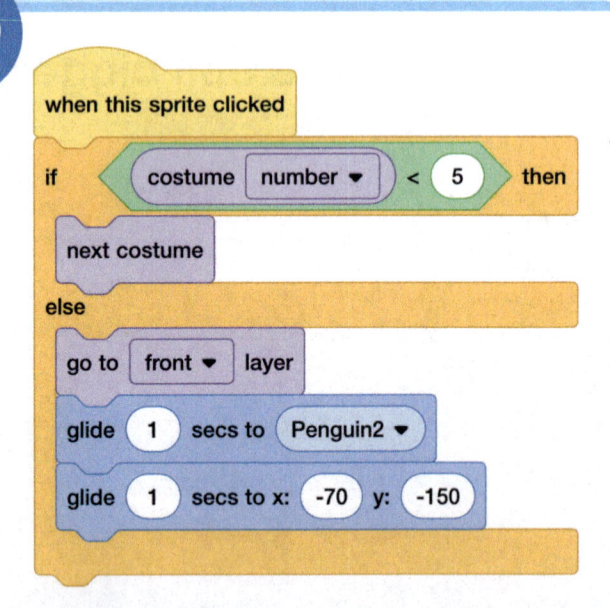

```
when [flag] clicked
go to x: -70 y: -150
switch costume to Gift4
```

10
```
when this sprite clicked
if < costume number < 5 > then
    next costume
else
    go to front layer
    glide 1 secs to Penguin2
    glide 1 secs to x: -70 y: -150
```

Add code to unwrap the present each time it is clicked.

When the present is unwrapped you can play catch with a penguin!

70

Answers

Day 2 Wordsearch

E	G	N	I	S	N	E	S	E	D	D	Y
R	Q	A	Z	L	M	W	C	D	H	Z	B
S	E	J	R	U	K	L	P	O	D	R	X
N	Q	P	T	E	I	Y	A	C	B	Y	M
O	P	S	E	C	T	S	P	R	I	T	E
W	O	E	K	A	D	N	A	Q	J	O	E
C	R	L	S	T	T	N	I	R	S	G	W
L	D	K	S	K	D	Y	X	W	A	M	W
B	K	R	J	O	N	Q	V	T	T	V	Y
S	C	A	M	Q	O	L	S	K	I	F	A
U	A	P	E	N	G	U	I	N	V	Z	K
W	B	S	E	H	T	C	E	J	O	R	P

The 5 elves were on pages 3, 20, 30, 68 and 72

Day 23 '10' differences

Day 6 Find the costumes

Muffin · Bananas · Drums Tabla · Laptop · Glow-T · Hat1

Day 16 Find the stars

Costumes

Backdrops

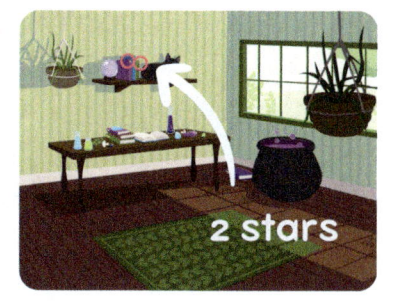

2 stars

71

Add your own style by changing **colours** and **costumes**

What next?

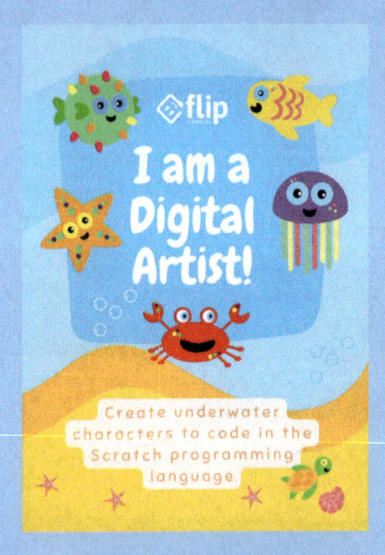

I am a Digital Artist!
Create underwater characters to code in the Scratch programming language

I am a Digital Artist!
Create space themed characters to code in the Scratch programming language

Available at Amazon

Index page

5	Day 1 – Chirp		35	Day 13 – Draw a snowball
7	Day 2 – Northern lights		37	Day 14 – Shooting star
11	Day 3 – Drag a star		39	Day 15 – Find the coin
13	Day 4 – Jump!		41	Day 16 – Star trail
15	Day 5 – I ❤ winter		45	Day 17 – Snowball splat
17	Day 6 – Draw a face		49	Day 18 – Tree lights
21	Day 7 – Hide		51	Day 19 – Draw a bow
23	Day 8 – Dress up		55	Day 20 – More balloons
25	Day 9 – Music		57	Day 21 – Star costumes
27	Day 10 – Draw a balloon		61	Day 22 – Snowflakes
31	Day 11 – Starry night		63	Day 23 – Build a snowman
33	Day 12 – Slide		67	Day 24 – Unwrap the gift

Printed in Great Britain
by Amazon